Praise for *Teaching with Heart*

"I wish I could afford to buy copies of *Teaching with Heart* for all the teachers I have interviewed in my forty years of reporting. My budget can't handle that. Instead, I recommend that all of us non-teachers buy copies of this inspiring book for teachers we know. You will probably want one for yourself, too."

—John Merrow, education correspondent,
PBS NewsHour; president, Learning Matters, Inc.

"*Teaching with Heart* is the rarest kind of book: one that actually does justice to the full range of emotion and skill teaching requires. These remarkable poems, selected by teachers and accompanied by their moving commentaries, provide a personal and powerful antidote to the caricatures and misperceptions we often see in headlines or popular culture, and speak to the heart of the teaching experience."

—Wendy Kopp, founder, Teach For America;
chief executive officer, Teach For All

"Although we understand that teaching is an intellectual activity, we also understand that it is a moral activity. To do it well, great teachers engage both the mind and the heart. *Teaching with Heart* portrays that wonderful combination of the heart and mind."

—Gloria Ladson-Billings, Kellner Family Chair
in Urban Education, University of Wisconsin–Madison

"At its best, teaching is like poetry: it inspires, challenges, and transforms. In this exhilarating collection, ninety teachers use poetry to illustrate the ups, downs, joys, frustrations, and, ultimately, the redeeming value of both teaching and poetry.

In spite of the increasing demands on teachers, the disrespect with which they're treated, and the appalling conditions in which so many work, these teachers, and millions of others, continue to practice their craft with courage, hope, and love. This book will be a bedside companion to teachers who need to know they are our nation's unsung treasure, as well as a wake-up call to the nation about the value of its teachers."

—Sonia Nieto, professor emerita, University of Massachusetts, Amherst; author of *Finding Joy in Teaching Students of Diverse Backgrounds: Culturally Responsive and Socially Just Practices in U.S. Schools*

"As a poet and a teacher, I'm always looking for what is essential and how it can be of use. In *Teaching with Heart*, you will find both food and tools for anyone who wants to learn or teach. It inspires and models the use of what matters in life and community. A must for any classroom."

—Mark Nepo, author of *The Book of Awakening* and *Seven Thousand Ways to Listen*

"'Warn the whole Universe that your heart can no longer live without real love.' Those words from the poet Hafiz are the reason you must buy this book, as the best possible field guide to accompany you through the brambles, over the chasms, up and down the treacherous slopes that every teacher with heart traverses every day of the year, while carrying society's most sacred trust."

—Diana Chapman Walsh, president emerita, Wellesley College

Teaching with Heart

POETRY THAT SPEAKS TO THE COURAGE TO TEACH

SAM M. INTRATOR AND MEGAN SCRIBNER, EDITORS

FOREWORD BY PARKER J. PALMER
INTRODUCTION BY TAYLOR MALI
AFTERWORD BY SARAH BROWN WESSLING

JB JOSSEY-BASS™
A Wiley Brand

Jacket design by Adrian Morgan
Cover photograph © Toa55 | Thinkstock (RF)

The credit lines beginning on page 245 constitute a continuation of this copyright page.

Published by Jossey-Bass
A Wiley Brand
One Montgomery Street, Suite 1200, San Francisco, CA 94104-4594—www.josseybass.com

Jossey-Bass books and products are available through most bookstores. To contact Jossey-Bass directly call our Customer Care Department within the U.S. at 800-956-7739, outside the U.S. at 317-572-3986, or fax 317-572-4002.

Wiley publishes in a variety of print and electronic formats and by print-on-demand. Some material included with standard print versions of this book may not be included in e-books or in print-on-demand. If this book refers to media such as a CD or DVD that is not included in the version you purchased, you may download this material at http://booksupport.wiley.com. For more information about Wiley products, visit www.wiley.com.

Library of Congress Cataloging-in-Publication Data is on file.

ISBN 978-1-118-45943-0 (hardcover)

Printed in the United States of America
FIRST EDITION
HB Printing 10 9 8 7 6 5 4 3 2 1

Contents

A Note to Our Readers by Sam M. Intrator and Megan Scribner   xi

Foreword by Parker J. Palmer   xxi

Introduction by Taylor Mali   xxvii

Relentless Optimism   1

Emma Lazarus's **"The New Colossus"** reflection by Randi Weingarten   2

Fleet Foxes' **"Helplessness Blues"** reflection by Stephen Lazar   4

Marianne Williamson's **"A Return to Love"** [Excerpt] reflection by
    Rachel Willis   6

Edgar Lee Masters's **"George Gray"** reflection by Mel Glenn   8

Robert Frost's **"The Road Not Taken"** reflection by Kaitlin Roig   10

Rudyard Kipling's **"IF"** reflection by Andy Wood   12

Loris Malaguzzi's **"No Way. The Hundred is There."**
    reflection by Tiffany Poirier   14

Gerald Jonas's **"Lessons"** reflection by Julie A. Gorlewski   16

Taylor Mali's **"What Teachers Make"** reflection by Kevin Hodgson   18

Teachable Moments 21

Rainier Maria Rilke's **"All will come again into its strength"**
reflection by Gregory John   22

Richard Wilbur's **"The Writer"** reflection by Emily Brisse   24

Theodore Roethke's **"The Waking"** reflection by Nora Landon   26

Emily Dickinson's **"'Tis so much joy! 'Tis so much joy!"**
reflection by Lily Eskelsen García   28

Paul Boswell's **"This Splendid Speck"** reflection by Christine Intagliata   30

Stanley Kunitz's **"Halley's Comet"** reflection by Rob Maitra   32

Emily Dickinson's **"If I can stop one Heart from breaking"**
reflection by Annette Breaux   34

John O'Donohue's **"Beannacht"** reflection by Emanuel Pariser   36

D. H. Lawrence's **"The Best of School"** reflection by Tom Vander Ark   38

Beauty in the Ordinary 41

Fernando Pessoa's **"To Be Great, Be Entire"** reflection by Vicki Den Ouden   42

Naomi Shihab Nye's **"Famous"** reflection by Safaa Abdel-Magid   44

Pablo Neruda's **"In Praise of Ironing"** reflection by Cindy O'Donnell-Allen   46

Louise Glück's **"Aubade"** reflection by Kent Dickson   48

W. H. Auden's **"In Memory of W. B. Yeats"** [Excerpt] reflection by
Jamie Raskin   50

Stephen Crane's **"LVIII"** reflection by Liam Corley   52

Mary Oliver's **"Crossing the Swamp"** reflection by Maureen Geraghty   54

Philip Levine's **"What Work Is"** reflection by Holly Masturzo   56

Walt Whitman's **"Section II from 'Song of Myself'"** reflection by Jennifer
Boyden   58

Enduring Impact   61

Naomi Shihab Nye's **"Kindness"** reflection by Hannah Cushing   62

Margaret Atwood's **"You Begin"** reflection by Karen Harris   64

Thich Nhat Hanh's **"Please Call Me by My True Names"**
reflection by Ruth Charney   66

William Stafford's **"Deciding"** reflection by Michael Poutiatine   68

Li-Young Lee's **"Eating Together"** reflection by Wanda S. Praisner   70

John O'Donohue's **"Blessing: For Presence"** reflection by David Henderson   72

Tara Sophia Mohr's **"Your Other Name"** reflection by Lianne Raymond   74

Jim R. Rogers's **"Good Morning!"** reflection by Jane Zalkin   76

Galway Kinnell's **"Saint Francis and the Sow"**
reflection by Kirsten Olson   78

The Work Is Hard   81

Antonio Machado's **"VI"** reflection by Michael L. Crauderueff   82

Mary Oliver's **"Wild Geese"** reflection by Kathleen Melville   84

Calvin Coolidge's **"Persistence"** reflection by April Niemela   86

Sharon Olds's **"On the Subway"** reflection by Lori Ungemah   88

Anonymous's **"Work Gloves"** reflection by Tom Meyer   90

William Stafford's **"Next Time"** reflection by Leanne Grabel Sander   92

Emily Dickinson's **"We grow accustomed to the Dark—"**
reflection by Rachel Fentin   94

Walt Whitman's **"When I Heard the Learn'd Astronomer"**
· reflection by Ronald Gordon   96

Wislawa Szymborska's **"Life While-You-Wait"** reflection by Veta Goler   98

Tenacity   101

Tupac Shakur's **"The Rose That Grew from Concrete"**
reflection by Jose Vilson   102

Philip Levine's **"M. Degas Teaches Art & Science at Durfee Intermediate School, Detroit, 1942"** reflection by Laura Roop   104

Mel King's **"Struggle"** reflection by Susan Rodgerson   106

Langston Hughes's **"Theme for English B"** reflection by Paola Tineo   108

Irene Rutherford McLeod's **"Lone Dog"** reflection by LouAnne Johnson   110

Billy Collins's **"On Turning Ten"** reflection by Will Bangs   112

Edgar A. Guest's **"It Couldn't Be Done"** reflection by Glendean Hamilton   114

Lao-Tzu's **"On Leadership"** reflection by Larry Rosenstock   116

William Ernest Henley's **"Invictus"** reflection by Caridad Caro   118

Feisty   121

Rumi's **"Out beyond ideas of wrongdoing and rightdoing"**
reflection by Hugh Birdsall   122

Mary Oliver's **"The Poet Dreams of the Classroom"**
reflection by Katie Johnson   124

Langston Hughes's **"Mother to Son"** reflection by Ron Walker   126

Jane Kenyon's **"Otherwise"** reflection by Alison Overseth   128

Richard Brautigan's **"The Memoirs of Jessie James"**
reflection by Stephen Mahoney   130

Marge Piercy's **"To be of use"** reflection by Amy Christie   132

Maya Angelou's **"Still I Rise"** reflection by Mary Beth Hertz   134

Olive Senior's **"Colonial Girls School"** reflection by Dena Simmons   136

The Freedom Writers with Erin Gruwell's **"An Innocent Freedom Writer"**
   reflection by Kayleigh Colombero   138

Moment to Moment   141

Bill Holm's **"Advice"** reflection by Teri O'Donnell   142

Katha Pollitt's **"Lilacs in September"** reflection by David S. Goldstein   144

Herman Hesse's **"The Ferryman"** reflection by Rachel Boechler   146

Mark Nepo's **"The Appointment"** reflection by Judy Sorum Brown   148

Captain Ed Davidson's **"Footprints by the Sea"** reflection by
   Sandi Bisceglia   150

Rumi's **"The Guest House"** reflection by Richard H. Ackerman   152

Chuang Tzu's **"Flight from the Shadow"** reflection by Mark Bielang   154

Thomas Merton's **"In Silence"** reflection by Thomas A. Stewart   156

Derek Walcott's **"Love After Love"** reflection by Tim Ryan   158

Together   161

John Daniel's **"A Prayer among Friends"** reflection by Melissa Madenski   162

Maya Angelou's **"Alone"** reflection by Nina Ashur   164

Stephen Dunn's **"The Sacred"** reflection by Dan Mindich   166

James A. Autry's **"On Firing A Salesman"** reflection by Brian Dixon   168

Robert Herrick's **"To the Virgins, to make much of Time"**
   reflection by Cordell Jones   170

Lucille Clifton's **"blessing the boats"** reflection by Kathleen Glaser   172

Raymond Carver's **"Happiness"** reflection by Dennis Huffman   174

X. J. Kennedy's **"Little Elegy"** reflection by Kenneth Rocke   176

Mel Glenn's **"A Teacher's Contract"** reflection by Harriet Sanford   178

Called to Teach   181

Gary Snyder's **"For the Children"** reflection by Julia Hill   182

Maya Angelou's **"The Lesson"** reflection by Jovan Miles   184

Gregory Orr's **"It's not magic; it isn't a trick"** reflection by John Mayer   186

Judy Sorum Brown's **"Hummingbirds asleep"** reflection by Sandie Merriam   188

John Fox's **"When Someone Deeply Listens to You"** reflection
   by Nell Etheredge   190

Alexis Rotella's **"Purple"** reflection by Leatha Fields-Carey   192

William Stafford's **"The Way It Is"** reflection by Donna Y. Chin   194

Langston Hughes's **"I loved my friend"** reflection by Margaret Wilson   196

Wendell Berry's **"The Real Work"** reflection by Amy Harter   198

Using Poetry for Reflection and Conversation   201

Afterword by Sarah Brown Wessling   221

Center for Courage & Renewal   223

The Contributors   225

The Editors   241

Gratitudes   243

Credits   245

A Note to Our Readers

*T*he late avant-garde composer John Cage was famous for his iconoclastic creations. Perhaps his most notorious work is his composition *4'33"*, which was performed in 1952 by pianist David Tudor, who sat at a piano without playing a note for four and a half minutes. Cage was also a prolific watercolorist, and his canvases have been exhibited throughout the world. The caveat he imposed on museum curators, who are accustomed to agonizing over the precise order and arrangement of visual art in an exhibition, was that they had to roll a dice to determine the order of the prints in homage to Cage's principle of "chance operations."[1]

When we worked on *Teaching with Fire* over ten years ago and then on *Leading from Within*, the first two volumes in this series, we operated with "anti-Cage" editorial principles. We fussed and wrestled with the order of the poems and stories to create a coherent metanarrative. In *Teaching with Fire*, after much give-and-take and many drafts, we decided to open the book with Bob O'Meally's poem that begins, "Make music with your life," and ends with the image, "walk thru azure sadness / howlin / Like a guitar player."[2]

---

1. M. Allen, "Taubman Curators Roll Dice to Arrange Upcoming John Cage Exhibition," *Arts & Extras* (blog), *Roanoke Times*, February 1, 2013, http://blogs.roanoke.com/arts/2013/02/taubman-curators-roll-dice-to-arrange-upcoming-john-cage-exhibition/#sthash.ej6UWwJE.dpuf.

2. S. M. Intrator and M. Scribner, *Teaching with Fire: Poetry That Sustains the Courage to Teach* (San Francisco: Jossey-Bass, 2003), 2.

We began with this "noisy image" because it celebrated a theme coursing through the teachers' submissions. Teachers described how the teaching life is busy, unpredictable, and filled with challenges. It requires a spirit for improvisation that, as John J. Sweeney wrote, happens "in little chairs . . . reading, writing, drawing, and playing guitar."[3]

In working on this book, we still heard teachers describe the vital and creative passion they have for their work, and we read commentaries in which they portrayed teaching as a form of artistry alive with opportunities for aesthetic discretion and playfulness. But the general tenor of responses suggested that conditions have changed for teachers. The writing we received described how mandates and prescriptions at the school and district levels have affected how teachers teach and how they experience the profession. They attributed this formidable change to the prioritization of testing and accountability policies and an accompanying obsession with "data." Teachers experience this as a narrowing of their creative autonomy and a discounting of their professional expertise. As one veteran teacher said, "I may make music, but it's feeling less like the improvisational jazz that marked how I thought about my work when I was young and more like muzak."

Maybe we shouldn't be surprised. The process of collecting and analyzing data has become ubiquitous in our lives. Our consumer preferences, health information, online personas, and more are collected into databases where complex algorithms analyze our trends. As the *New York Times* columnist David Brooks observed, "If you asked me to describe the rising philosophy of the day, I'd say it is data-ism. We now have the ability to gather huge amounts of data. This ability seems to carry with it certain cultural assumptions—that everything that can be measured should be measured; that data is a transparent and reliable lens that

---

3. Intrator and Scriber, *Teaching with Fire*, 2.

A Note to Our Readers

allows us to filter out emotionalism and ideology; that data will help us do remarkable things."[4]

Perhaps nowhere more than in education has the belief that "collecting and analyzing data will help us do remarkable things"gained momentum. The field has systematically moved to data-driven instruction, value-added evaluation, and other structures that attempt to pinpoint and coordinate objective and scientific educational practices that produce student learning. It's an approach whereby all various data, such as standardized test scores, dropout figures, percentages of non-native speakers proficient in English, and so on, are collected and disaggregated by ethnicity and school grade, and analyzed. The rationale for collecting this expansive trove of data was explained by the noted education historian Larry Cuban: "With access to data warehouses, staff can obtain electronic packets of student performance data that can be used to make instructional decisions to increase academic performance. Data-driven instruction, advocates say, is scientific and consistent with how successful businesses have used data for decades in making decisions that increased their productivity."[5]

These macrolevel changes, driven by technological trends and accelerated by policy and legislation such as No Child Left Behind, the Race to the Top initiative, and the design of the Common Core State Standards, have formatively altered the microexperience of teaching. What the outcomes of this shift have been in regard to improving student achievement and identifying specific procedures and pedagogies is still a live question. What we do know, according to Cuban, is that "now, principals and teachers are awash in data."[6]

---

4. D. Brooks, "The Philosophy of Data," *New York Times*, February 4, 2013.

5. L. Cuban, "Data-Driven Instruction and the Practice of Teaching," *Larry Cuban on School Reform and Classroom Practice* (blog), May 12, 2011, http://larrycuban.wordpress.com/2011/05/12/data-driven -instruction-and-the-practice-of-teaching/.

6. Cuban, "Data-Driven Instruction."

In addition, the submissions we received conveyed that the day-to-day stresses and pressures on teachers take their toll. More and more teachers feel that they are expected to make up for the ills of society and the flagging ability of many of our nation's children to achieve. Teachers face excessive demands on their time; they work with students often wounded by trauma or pulled down and apart by the punishing toll of poverty; they feel undermined by policy mandates or by the presence of accountability regimes that narrow their creative discretion as teachers; and they struggle with a sense of loneliness that comes from working in an institution that provides little collaborative time and has meager norms of collegial interaction.

Yet despite these challenges and the profound shifts in the context of where and how they teach, the enduring story teachers tell about their work remains constant. Teachers believe in the exuberant potential and possibility of their work. They have a deep, abiding, and passionate sense of vocation. They come to teaching to work with children, to serve society, led by the conviction that through education we can move individuals and society to a more promising future. These core and animating principles draw people into the work, but they become tempered over time as teachers run into the obstacles and forces at work in our classrooms, schools, and culture.

In this book, teachers describe the rhythms and meaning of their work and lives through stories and poems. It is fitting, as the power of story runs through the profession. In fact, we have always believed that if James Joyce were to write a sequel to *Ulysses*—his sprawling, stream-of-consciousness, detail-thick novel that chronicles eighteen episodes in the day of Leopold Bloom—he could write about a teacher's life. The buzzing complexity of the classroom, the enlarged meaning of seemingly humdrum details, and the drama of so many individual and collective stories playing out in the learning and lives of students would make a suitable subject for a complex and layered novel. As Maxine Greene observed, at all levels of teaching and schools, "the sounds of storytelling are everywhere."[7]

---

7. M. Greene, "Foreword," in *Stories Lives Tell: Narrative and Dialogue in Education*, ed. C. Witherell & N. Noddings (New York: Teachers College Press, 1991), x.

A Note to Our Readers

Stories help give meaning to our lives; define who we are; illuminate our relationships to others; and, as the philosopher Charles Taylor (1989) has told us, guide our future actions by highlighting where we stand in relation to our commitments. Stories help us to determine "from case to case what is good, or valuable, or what ought to be done, or what [one] endorses or opposes."[8] In other words, stories locate us in our present moment and shape our journey.

In this book, the teachers share revelations about their teaching life and their encounters with poems that have meant something to them. We believe poetry is particularly apt for this sort of examination, as poetry compresses meaning into charged particles of language and image. Poetry stirs up an inner conversation about questions, emotions, and things that matter. Because poetry slows us down and focuses our attention, it can yield poignant insights into what is most significant and enduring in our work as educators. It is a different form of "big data," one that William Blake understood when he wrote:

> To see a World in a Grain of Sand
> And a Heaven in a Wild Flower,
> Hold Infinity in the palm of your hand
> And Eternity in an hour.[9]

We sent out the call for submissions through emails, websites, networks, and conversations with colleagues, family, and friends. We contacted organizations involved in programs working with teachers, poetry, or both, including those that profiled and supported remarkable teachers. We told educators that this book would seek to provide a platform for teachers and educators to speak wholeheartedly about the teaching life and the challenges and possibilities that teachers

---

8. C. Taylor, *Sources of the Self: The Making of the Modern Identity* (Cambridge, MA: Harvard University Press, 1989), 27.

9. W. Blake, *The Complete Poetry and Prose of William Blake* (New York: Random House, 1988), 490.

encounter every day in their work. We asked them to submit a favorite poem and a brief personal story (250 words) that described why this particular poem held meaning for them, personally or professionally.

We were honored and overwhelmed by the outpouring of submissions for the book. We received hundreds of poignant responses from educators. Each commentary and poem shared a compelling perspective on teaching and education. We were moved by the stories—heartfelt reflections that painted a picture of the formidable challenges teachers face day in and day out—and by the intelligence, heart, passion and courage these individuals bring to their chosen profession. It was also a pleasure to hear how many found the process of writing their reflection rewarding in and of itself. One of our contributors, Jennifer Boyden, wrote: "I want to thank you not just for the opportunity to submit, but also for the conversation this has opened up with my friends and me as we have selected poems, thought about them, and discussed what we're up to." And Melissa Madenski, a middle school teacher, wrote: "Whatever happens, to go through this process [of reflecting on a poem] is a good one for any teacher!"

The editorial board carefully reviewed the submissions, selecting the entries for the book using criteria that included the quality of the poem, the story behind each poem, and how these poems and stories would work together to form a cohesive whole that would represent the wide range of teachers' perspectives and experiences.

We are delighted with the broad array of educators represented by these ninety submissions. They embody the many faces and contexts of teaching: preschool, elementary school, middle school, and high school. They work in a variety of institutional settings and schools: public; charter; independent; four-year colleges; community colleges; universities; and out-of-school settings, such as afterschool programs. They hail from across the continuum of experience, from aspiring teachers, to novices, to midcareer veterans, to retired teachers. They teach online, in classrooms, in cities and small towns, and through such leadership roles as principals of schools, leaders of unions, or superintendents of districts.

Encountering the array of perspectives from these educators was a wonderful aspect of this work.

What is clear—no matter the background, level of experience, position, or context—is that all of these educators strive faithfully to honor the noble aspirations of their profession. They believe that the *real work of teaching* is an art form that when performed well encompasses skill, judgment, imagination, strategic planning, improvisational fluidity, and the highest levels of intelligence. The country is fortunate to have such dedicated professionals teaching in our nation's schools and offering support to our students and fellow educators. We count ourselves lucky to have had this opportunity to work with them and feature them in this book.

In the course of describing our efforts, we often said, "This is not your typical poetry anthology." Most anthologies singularly focus on the quality of poetry and the relationship of poetry to a particular theme. For example, one of our most treasured anthologies is Czeslaw Milosz's *A Book of Luminous Things*. It's a collection of three hundred poems that were selected because they render the emotional and physical realities of the world palpable, singular, and immediate. They are of luminosity. Milosz wrote that he assembled the anthology while he was in Berkeley, and he described how he uncovered the "hoard" of poems. "Berkeley has, probably, the best bookstores in America, and also good libraries, including the libraries of theological schools of various denominations. . . [It] possesses a quite high density of poets per square mile. As a consequence of all this, its bookstores afford a good opportunity to browse in poetry."[10]

Our approach has been fundamentally different. We have collected and arranged poems that teachers indicated were poignant and meaningful to them. The result of this work is that we have an eclectic collection that stretches across centuries, cultures, and genres.

---

10. C. Miłosz, *A Book of Luminous Things: An International Anthology of Poetry* (New York: Houghton Mifflin Harcourt, 1998), xvi.

In the spirit of offering *Teaching with Heart* poetry trivia, we can share that after Emily Dickinson, the poet most submitted to the selection process was Mary Oliver, and then William Stafford. The poem most submitted (six teachers sent in commentaries) was "The Writer" by Richard Wilbur. We may not have scoured the bookstores like Milosz, but we too found a rich source for poems, as each day we were fortunate to find our email full of poems and submissions sent by teachers. We browsed the poetic world in a different way.

The stories and poetry in the book are organized into ten sections that tell a broad-ranging story from the teacher's perspective about the project of American education. Following these ten sections is a short resource section on how poetry can support teachers in their work.

The first section of stories and poetry, "Relentless Optimism," considers how despite facing myriad draining demands and pressures, teachers find ways to believe in the promise of teaching and keep a spirit of optimism alive.

"Teachable Moments" homes in on moments of wonder within a teacher's life and work. Commentaries in this section describe episodes in which the "lightbulb" goes off and illuminates the inside of a classroom—and powerful learning transpires.

"Beauty in the Ordinary" and "Enduring Impact" describe how teachers, although awash in a sea of data and quantitative representations of what constitutes learning, still find enduring satisfaction from the intensely human and relational aspects of their work.

"The Work Is Hard" and "Tenacity" contend with those forces that can demoralize teachers: testing, high rates of poverty among students, intensified scrutiny around test scores, large class sizes, and other depleting challenges. These sections look at how to meet these challenges both within and outside the classroom.

In "Feisty," "Moment to Moment," and "Together," teachers look at what they can do, both as individuals and as colleagues, to resist the status quo and create inspiring new ways to teach, learn, and work with students. Part of this is acknowledging that they will not always hit the ball out of the park, and part of it is recognizing and accepting their imperfections. These educators also describe how they take care of themselves and note the importance of adult relationships in schools in helping them sustain their engagement in their work.

And finally, in "Called to Teach," teachers describe their abiding relationship to teaching as a vocation. They depict teaching as a calling—and despite the challenges, they believe that what they do matters. Their words are evidence of the almost inexplicable, relentless optimism of teachers—for which we're very grateful.

Sam M. Intrator
Megan Scribner
May 2014

Foreword

Parker J. Palmer

It is difficult
to get the news from poems
    yet men die miserably every day
        for lack
of what is found there.

        —William Carlos Williams

Teaching with Heart is full of good news about our schools. This news comes not from the mass media, which carry an endless stream of bad-news stories about American education—or, more precisely, about the political football American education has become. The good news comes from ninety gifted and committed educators, each of whom shares a brief personal story about the teaching life, accompanied by a poem that embodies insights, values, or a vision that helps sustain him or her. These stories and poems take us inside the heart of a teacher and offer proof positive that our school-age children are in the care of many competent, compassionate, committed, and courageous adults.

For the past quarter century, I've had the privilege of working with thousands of teachers across the United States. I can testify from personal experience that the contributors to this book are not random miracles in their oft-maligned profession.

They represent countless unheralded professionals who give endlessly of themselves to help their students fulfill the potential that every child possesses. The miracle is that so many teachers like these have found ways to sustain themselves in a profession that we depend on and yet denigrate on a daily basis.

If we are fully to appreciate the courage that keeps these teachers returning to their post, we have to understand the impact of the bad news about American education—which brings us back to the mass media. The *New York Times* recently reported that in a reputable survey of teacher morale, "more than half of teachers expressed at least some reservation about their jobs, their highest level of dissatisfaction since 1989. . . Also, roughly one in three said they were likely to leave the profession in the next five years, citing concerns over job security, as well as the effects of increased class size and deep cuts to services and programs. Just three years ago, the rate was one in four."[1]

Statistics of that sort are brought to life by a million anecdotes like this one. A friend of mine recently learned that her son, who had always loved math, was doing poorly in his fifth-grade math course. "That class is so boring," he told his mom. "Every day our teacher writes our homework on the board and makes us write it down so we can take it home." When my friend asked the teacher why she took up valuable classroom time with such a primitive practice, the answer was simple: "Because the school can't afford to xerox the homework handouts, and neither can I."

Here's another statistic about what American teachers and their students are up against. An appalling one-fifth of the children in this country—that's sixteen million kids—come from food-insecure households, and two-thirds of American teachers "regularly see kids who show up at school hungry because they aren't getting enough to eat at home."[2] Every day, teachers in this affluent country are

---

1. F. Santos, "Teacher Survey Shows Morale Is at a Low Point," *New York Times*, March 7, 2012, http://www.nytimes.com/2012/03/08/education/teacher-morale-sinks-survey-results-show.html.

2. "Hunger Facts," Share Our Strength, accessed January 15, 2014, http://www.nokidhungry.org/problem/hunger-facts.

reaching into their own pockets to buy food for some of their students, to say noth-
ing of basic school supplies their students need that their school cannot afford.

Then, of course, there are the "high-stakes" tests that do little to improve the
quality of American education but cause widespread grief, all for the sake of help-
ing politicians look "serious" about public education. Our obsession with testing is
punishing teachers whose students don't get on base, even when those students
began with two strikes against them, making teachers and students alike feel like
failures in the process. It is creating a culture of "teaching to the test" that leaves
no room for the open-ended exploring that real education requires. It is pushing
important subjects like art and music out of the curriculum because their "learning
outcomes" can't be measured quantitatively. And it is driving many good teachers
out of the profession because they are being told to put test scores ahead of their
students' real needs.

To add insult to injury, teachers are often used by politicians, the press, and
the public as scapegoats for a raft of problems that teachers did not create and
cannot solve, at least not by themselves. People complain endlessly about "all
those incompetent teachers" who turn out children with subpar skills in reading,
writing, and arithmetic. But the root cause of many children's failure to learn is *not*
poor teaching. It is poverty and the way it deprives children of the resources they
need—from adequate nutrition to strong adult support—to succeed at school.[3]

Against that bad-news backdrop, let's get back to the good news that is rein-
forced on every page of this book: American teachers are our "culture heroes," the
true "first responders" to societal problems that "We the People" and our political
leaders lack the wit or the will to solve, problems that show up first in the lives of
the vulnerable young.

Despite poor working conditions, teachers show up at school every day with
welcoming smiles and thoughtful lesson plans developed on weekends and by the

---

3. David Sarota, "New Data Shows School 'Reformers' Are Full of It," June 3, 2013, http://www.salon
.com/2013/06/03/instead_of_a_war_on_teachers_how_about_one_on_poverty/.

midnight oil. Despite the fact that they're often underpaid and their schools are underfinanced, they do their work with full hearts, faithfully, and well. Despite the drumbeat of "accountability" that puts test scores above all else, they never forget that their ultimate responsibility is to this child, and this child, and this child. Despite the fact that they are surrounded by public misunderstanding and political interventions, they keep investing themselves in the promise with which every child is born.

Where do teachers find the resources necessary to continue to serve our children in such difficult circumstances? In the two places where people of conscience and commitment have always found the power to resist and transform external circumstances that might otherwise defeat the best of human possibilities. They find it within themselves, *in the human heart*. And they find it between themselves, *in communities of mutual support*.

For millennia, poetry has helped our species evoke, nurture, and sustain the human heart and connect with each other in supportive communities. So the poems that accompany the teaching stories in this book are more, much more, than grace notes. From the nonverbal poetry of the paintings in the Lascaux Caves (estimated to be more than seventeen thousand years old), through ancient texts of wisdom traditions around the world, to the work of contemporary poets, poetry has given human beings a way to tap into insights and energies that allow us to keep our finest aspirations alive and come together in the endless struggle to achieve them.

To take but one example from this book (spoiler alert), look at the entry by seventh-grade teacher Annette Breaux. From her first day of teaching, Annette has had a poem by Emily Dickinson on her desk, a poem that begins, "If I can stop one Heart from breaking, / I shall not live in vain." One day she discussed that poem with her students, and sent them home with a simple assignment: "Do something nice for someone." When you learn what that assignment did for a student named Thomas and his mother, and for Annette, you will know what I mean when I say that poetry has the power to arouse the human heart and help create communities of mutual support.

William Carlos Williams got it right when he wrote the poem with which this foreword begins: "It is difficult / to get the news from poems / yet men die miserably every day / for lack / of what is found there." For millennia, men and women have been turning that truth around by relying on poetry for news that is life giving and empowering, as the stories in this book demonstrate.

In the mass media, today's bad-news stories about American education will be old news tomorrow. Of course, we cannot ignore these stories—they point toward problems we need to solve if we want our teachers to have the support they need to keep serving our children well. But we who care about education, and those teachers whose work we value, must find sources of sustenance for the long haul, and poetry provides some of what we need.

Unlike the stories told in the mass media, the stories told by poetry will not be old news tomorrow. "Literature is news that stays news," said the poet Ezra Pound, because it taps into the bottomless resources of human community and the human heart.[4] For that—and for all the competent, compassionate, committed, and courageous teachers in our schools—we can give great thanks.

Parker J. Palmer, founder and senior partner of the Center for Courage & Renewal, is a well-known writer, speaker, and activist. He has reached millions worldwide through his nine books, including the best-selling *Let Your Life Speak, The Courage to Teach, A Hidden Wholeness*, and *Healing the Heart of Democracy*. He holds a PhD in sociology from the University of California at Berkeley, along with ten honorary doctorates, two Distinguished Achievement Awards from the National Educational Press Association, and an Award of Excellence from the Associated Church Press. In 2010 Parker was given the William Rainey Harper Award, whose previous recipients include Margaret Mead, Elie Wiesel, and Paolo Freire. In 2011 he was named an Utne Reader Visionary, one of "25 people who are changing your world."

---

4. E. Pound, *ABC of Reading* (1934; repr., New York: New Directions, 1960), 29.

Introduction

Taylor Mali

Toward the end of every summer, when the air begins to change, I can't help but count the years that have passed since I left the classroom as a regular teacher back in 2000. Part of me will always associate that quality of early-autumn air with the beginning of school, whether as a student or as a teacher.

In the Northeast, where I grew up, that time of year is a mixture of mown grass, cooler nights, and a smell I can only describe as *imminence*. Something about to start. As a student, I followed a yearly ritual to prepare for it: binders stocked full of loose-leaf; backpacks stuffed with pens and calculators; new clothes purchased; shots and immunizations obtained; and soccer practices attended, which, as a goaltender, I always dreaded just a little (glory, failure).

As a teacher, too, autumn meant it was time to get serious again, finish those lesson plans, put the schedules on the refrigerator, take a deep breath, and get ready for the onslaught: every student a striker on a mad breakaway heading straight for my goal.

Even after I quit my teaching job to see if I could pay the bills as a wandering poet and an itinerant creative writing consultant, the feeling of imminence that comes with the onset of early autumn never ebbed. My only job now, really, is to write and be on time for the readings and airplanes that have been set up for me. Yet each year in the last days of August, part of me starts thinking, *Summer's over. It's time to buckle down and go to school.*

For years I couldn't figure out why as a poet I still felt this way. But it makes perfect sense. Because on a very basic level, being a poet and being a teacher are inextricably linked. Whether teaching or writing, what I really am doing is shepherding revelation; I am the midwife to epiphany.

Consider this job description, attributed to the Roman poet Horace, who wrote during the time of Augustus: "The task of the poet is to either delight or instruct, and we must reserve our greatest approbation for those who can do both at the same time." Isn't that still true today? Aren't the best poems the ones that enchant us while teaching us something at the same time? And isn't that also the gift of the best teachers?

A teacher instructs, certainly—that's obvious—but the best teachers know intuitively that part of their job is to bring to the acquisition of knowledge and skills as much delight as possible. Students spend more time studying for the classes they care about—even though they may be challenging—than for the classes that bore them or don't seem to be relevant to their lives. A good teacher can capture their attention and imagination, and they can find themselves falling in love with the subject, sometimes in spite of themselves.

For a spoken-word poet, one whose work is written first for the ear rather than the eye, Horace's dictum is equally true. As I craft and rehearse my performances, I must not forget to delight, entertain, or even provoke my audience as I present my commentaries on the world. Trying to wrap whatever wisdom I might wring from my life lessons in beautiful turns of phrase and memorable imagery, I think often of the poet John Dryden, who may well have been channeling Horace when he wrote that "delight is the chief, if not the only, end of poetry; instruction can be admitted but in the second place, for poetry only instructs as it delights."[1]

---

1. J. Dryden, *An Essay of Dramatic Poesy*, 3rd ed., ed. T. Arnold, rev. by W. T. Arnold (Oxford, England: Clarendon Press, 1918), 104

All of this may help explain why a book like *Teaching with Heart* exists. Why so many teachers turn to poetry to sustain them, to remind them why they chose to do what they do, or simply to accompany them on their journey. There is something about the place whence good poetry springs—to say nothing of the places it can touch us or take us—that is familiar to the soul of the teacher. As I read the poems contained in this book, many of which I have known and loved myself for years, but *most* of which were new to me, that truth kept announcing itself to me over and over again: poetry replenishes the well because it is another way of teaching.

When I was a regular classroom teacher, I never once claimed to understand truly how anyone learns anything. And now that I'm a poet I still don't know. Sure, I've read the theories taught in colleges of education, and many of them make a lot of sense to me, especially Bloom's Taxonomy of Cognitive Domains. But there's still a lot of mystery surrounding how the brain works and how knowledge gets acquired, comprehended, applied, analyzed, and so on. Part of me is completely at ease with that mystery, that *not knowing*. It's the same part of me that loves poetry, I think, because poetry possesses mystery as well; as T. S. Eliot said, poetry can *communicate* before it is understood. But many policymakers who continually create new approaches to education have never been able to trust what they can't measure.[2]

The learned astronomer so enamored with "charts and diagrams" mentioned in Walt Whitman's poem, chosen and eloquently introduced by Ronald Gordon, a professor at the University of Hawai'i, is alive and well today and working in the US Department of Education, revealing through his prodigious mastery of policy and statistics his utter ignorance of actual teaching. Children, like the stars at the end of Whitman's poem, are distant, beautiful, and mysteriously rejuvenating. To believe this on the most basic level requires *gnosis*, an unexplainable knowledge akin to faith. As Ronald himself writes in wonderfully haphazard rhyme, "Heart,

---

2. T. S. Eliot, *The Selected Prose of T.S. Eliot*, ed. F. Kermode (Boston: Houghton Mifflin Harcourt, 1975), 206.

head, and hand united, we *reach*. And then, we *teach*." Not all the poetry in this book is to be found in a poem.

Of course, it's difficult to celebrate this spiritual, intuitive knowledge that all good teachers know exists but can't talk about without being laughed at or fired. And that's because the process of acquiring it can be as arduous as it is beautiful, as exhausting as it is transcendent. Wisdom is hard won, and not necessarily in the way you want it to be. Teaching is like "Crossing the Swamp," the Mary Oliver poem chosen and introduced by Maureen Geraghty, a high school teacher in Portland, Oregon, and as Maureen writes, the poem encourages her to "press on": "I read it often, especially when I want to give up and simply pass out work-sheets that fence off the swamp and deter any opportunities for engagement and interaction." Many other teachers have presented poems here that speak to the necessity of persistence, persistence despite not knowing all the answers or sometimes even feeling remotely ready or prepared. Where there is no path, you make one. And despite the desire to give up, you go on.

Why? Because teachers are famous. Maybe not to the world at large. Maybe not to history. But teachers can be famous to their students, as Safaa Abdel-Magid, a teacher at the Khartoum International Community School in Sudan, says in her discussion of "Famous" by Naomi Shihab Nye, just as "the tear is famous, briefly, to the cheek" (Nye). Our fame comes from our insistence that teaching is not a job we merely do but a thing we are. Or, as Vicki Den Ouden, a reading teacher in British Columbia, Canada, says, "To truly be great, [we] need to be like the moon— dependable and wholly present."

After my readings I often get asked whether I miss teaching. My stock answer is, "Never before seven in the morning," which is usually good for a laugh or two. Then I often launch into some version of what I wrote earlier in this introduction, describing how I feel as though I never stopped teaching, that I just traded in one classroom for another kind. "You can take the teacher out of the poem, but not the poetry out of the teacher," I say.

Sharing these sentiments usually satisfies the person who asked the question.

But sometimes, when something has broken me open a little (like reading the poems in this book and the stories written by the teachers who chose them) I answer this same question with a deeper honesty. Do I miss teaching? *Yes. Every single day.*

Taylor Mali is a spoken-word poet and a vocal advocate of teachers and the nobility of teaching, having himself spent nine years in the classroom teaching everything from English and history to math and SAT preparation. He is one of the most well-known poets to have emerged from the poetry slam movement and has performed and lectured for teachers all over the world. His twelve-year-long Quest for One Thousand Teachers, completed in April 2012, helped create one thousand new teachers through "poetry, persuasion, and perseverance." He is the author most recently of *What Teachers Make: In Praise of the Greatest Job in the World* as well as two books of poetry, *The Last Time as We Are* and *What Learning Leaves.*

Other books

Teaching with Fire
Sam M. Intrator and Megan Scribner, Editors

Leading from Within
Sam M. Intrator and Megan Scribner, Editors

The Quest for Mastery: Positive Youth Development
Through Out-of-School Programs
Sam M. Intrator and Don Siegel

The Heart of Higher Education: A Call to Renewal
Parker J. Palmer, Arthur Zajonc, and Megan Scribner

Living the Questions
Sam M. Intrator

Tuned In and Fired Up
Sam M. Intrator

Stories of the Courage to Teach
Sam M. Intrator

The Courage to Teach Guide for Reflection and Renewal
Parker J. Palmer and Megan Scribner

Teaching with Heart

Relentless Optimism

*I*n times of high anxiety over the economy, geopolitics, and social unrest, politicians, policymakers, and corporate leaders commission countless blue-ribbon reports that pundits use to sound the alarm about how our approach to schooling is undermining the economy and threatening our way of life.

Inside schools and classrooms, the teachers whom we know and who wrote for this book have little time, patience, or inclination for such pessimism and bleak projections. When school begins and teachers convene students for the start of a lesson or a class, pragmatism and optimism hold sway. Teachers ask themselves: *What will we learn, and how will I organize our time together?*

Teaching is work animated by hope and optimism. No matter the age or the subject taught, teachers believe that the work to be done in that classroom, in that moment, on that day, for that stretch of time has the possibility to irrevocably shape the future. They believe that the subjects they teach, the skills they impart, and the community values they cultivate can bend the very trajectories of individual lives.

The submissions in this book celebrate the spirit and courage of the 3.1 million teachers who each and every day, despite many challenges and obstacles, strive to "lift a lamp" in their classrooms.

I have been drawn to this poem—engraved on the pedestal of the Statue of Liberty—for as long as I can remember. Emma Lazarus invokes an iconic image—the Colossus of Rhodes—but she turns the image on its head. Unlike the "conquering" Colossus of old, this new Colossus is welcoming and embracing, beckoning all to our land of possibility. It's a New York poem (the "twin cities" refer to Manhattan and Brooklyn); it's about using power for good; and it's a hopeful poem, almost defiantly optimistic. Educators are fueled by such optimism—without which we couldn't do our work or instill hope in our students.

It's a nineteenth-century poem with twenty-first-century relevance. In public school classrooms across America, teachers educate and nurture students who are tired, poor, "tempest-tost," and yearning. Like Lazarus's inspiration, teachers lift their lamp and help fulfill our collective responsibility to enable individual opportunity for each and every child.

The Statue of Liberty—often called the "Immigrant's Statue"—serves as an inspiring reminder that America's essence has been shaped by immigrants. Although I am infuriated that some officials want to pull up the ladder behind them, I am heartened by the movement to combat that impulse and turn instead to fixing our immigration system. And I am proud of the students and educators in our public schools, which provide so many immigrants with opportunities for advancement and have done much to realize the vision of *e pluribus unum*—out of many, one.

—*Randi Weingarten*
President
American Federation of Teachers
Washington, DC

The New Colossus

Not like the brazen giant of Greek fame,
With conquering limbs astride from land to land;
Here at our sea-washed, sunset gates shall stand
A mighty woman with a torch, whose flame
Is the imprisoned lightning, and her name
Mother of Exiles. From her beacon-hand
Glows world-wide welcome; her mild eyes command
The air-bridged harbor that twin cities frame.
"Keep ancient lands, your storied pomp!" cries she
With silent lips. "Give me your tired, your poor,
Your huddled masses yearning to breathe free,
The wretched refuse of your teeming shore.
Send these, the homeless, tempest-tost to me,
I lift my lamp beside the golden door!"

—*Emma Lazarus*

In America, we are raised with Hollywood representations of the noble teacher who comes in and saves her students. These shining-knight moments do exist, but more often we are a small functioning cog in the greater machine of our students' lives.

Nine years in, despite great success by any measure in my classroom, I realize more and more each day how small is the role any individual teacher can play in the lives of students. A high school class is but one out of seven, one hour out of twenty-four, one year out of a lifetime.

It's been a long time since a song lyric meant anything to me. The lines that once haunted my thinking and filled any available space on my notebooks, lockers, and bedroom walls have faded over time. I don't even really hear the words in songs anymore. Living the cliché, then, of hearing a "song written for me" was quite a surprise for me on a January day in the middle of my hour-long subway ride to the Bronx.

The song is called "Helplessness Blues," yet hearing it made me feel neither helpless nor blue. When I heard it, a long-simmering epiphany finally came through: my successes in the classroom are never my own, but neither are my failures. The teacher is part of a school, which is part of a system, which is part of society. And without any one of us, everything would be different. Every cog fits together with the others, and matters.

—Stephen Lazar

High School History Teacher and Co-founder
Harvest Collegiate High School
New York, New York

Helplessness Blues

I was raised up believing I was somehow unique
Like a snowflake distinct among snowflakes, unique in each way you can see
And now after some thinking, I'd say I'd rather be
A functioning cog in some great machinery serving something beyond me

But I don't, I don't know what that will be
I'll get back to you someday soon you will see

What's my name, what's my station, oh, just tell me what I should do
I don't need to be kind to the armies of night that would do such injustice to you
Or bow down and be grateful and say "sure, take all that you see"
To the men who move only in dimly-lit halls and determine my future for me

And I don't, I don't know who to believe
I'll get back to you someday soon you will see

If I know only one thing, it's that everything that I see
Of the world outside is so inconceivable often I barely can speak
Yeah I'm tongue-tied and dizzy and I can't keep it to myself
What good is it to sing helplessness blues, why should I wait for anyone else?

And I know, I know you will keep me on the shelf
I'll come back to you someday soon myself

If I had an orchard, I'd work till I'm raw
If I had an orchard, I'd work till I'm sore
And you would wait tables and soon run the store

Gold hair in the sunlight, my light in the dawn
If I had an orchard, I'd work till I'm sore
If I had an orchard, I'd work till I'm sore
Someday I'll be like the man on the screen

—*The Fleet Foxes*

In many professions, when you get to the end of the day, you can shut off your mind and seamlessly switch to your personal life. These are professions that do not keep you awake at night strategizing new ways to reach a difficult student or concocting imaginative ways to teach the subject so it's fresh and new. These professions are more of a career and less of a calling.

Education is not one of those professions.

Nor is education just about the long hours we spend grading papers, crafting lesson plans, making phone calls to parents, speaking at PTA meetings, planning field trips, or tutoring students at the end of the day. Education is so much more than this.

The reason we lie awake at night is that what we do matters. We make readers, writers, mathematicians, and critical thinkers. We show students the ways of the world and inspire them to change it. We teach conflict resolution through playground games and prove that above all else, knowledge is power.

I truly believe that as educators, "we are powerful beyond measure." Yet sometimes we act as though we're "inadequate" and "play small"—this does not serve us or the world.

We *are* powerful beyond measure. In every lesson we teach, every decision we make, we are having an impact on the life outcomes of our students and generations of their families to follow. I love this passage from Marianne Williamson because it "liberates" me to embrace this power and shine as we are all meant to do.

—*Rachel Willis*

Director of Teacher and Alumni Leadership Development
Teach For America
Washington, DC

From "A Return to Love"

Our deepest fear is not that we are inadequate. Our deepest fear is that we are powerful beyond measure. It is our light, not our darkness, that most frightens us. We ask ourselves, Who am I to be brilliant, gorgeous, talented, and fabulous? Actually, who are you *not* to be? You are a child of God. Your playing small doesn't serve the world. There's nothing enlightened about shrinking so that other people will not feel insecure around you. We are all meant to shine, as children do. We were born to make manifest the glory of God that is within us. It's not just in some of us; it's in everyone. And as we let our own light shine, we unconsciously give other people permission to do the same. As we're liberated from our own fear, our presence automatically liberates others.

—*Marianne Williamson*

I live by the sea, five blocks from the water, two blocks from where Hurricane Sandy stopped. The salt of the sea is in my veins.

I've taught this poem many times, hoping to get students launched, to get them to take risks and not be afraid. George Gray worries from the grave about missed chances. Love, ambition, even sorrow knocked at his door, but he was afraid.

Adolescents are new, untested, bobbing boats. Their feelings are at war with everything and everyone. It is the teacher's task to guide these boats into the open waters of adulthood.

No matter the course, we must imbue them with meaning and purpose, for "life without meaning is the torture of restlessness and vague desire." But first we must get them and ourselves out of the harbor, and "lift the sail and catch the winds of destiny wherever they drive the boat." For as my favorite quote holds, "A ship in the harbor is safe—but that is not what ships are built for."[1]

I taught (thirty-one years) in the same school I attended. I was once one of those newly made ships, so I knew my school and my students fore and aft. Whether I was teaching *Macbeth* or *Catcher in the Rye*, or acting as a dean, essentially a counselor, there wasn't a problem I hadn't heard. I hope I encouraged my students to trust their own skills and judgment. Adolescence is hard enough; you need running lights.

—Mel Glenn

Retired High School English Teacher and Poet
Brooklyn, New York

---

1. J. Shedd, *Salt from My Attic* (Portland, ME: Mosher Press, 1928), 20.

George Gray

I HAVE studied many times
The marble which was chiseled for me—
A boat with a furled sail at rest in the harbor.
In truth it pictures not my destination
But my life.
For love was offered me and I shrank from its disillusionment;
Sorrow knocked at my door, but I was afraid;
Ambition called to me, but I dreaded the chances.
Yet all the while I hungered for meaning in my life.
And now I know we must lift the sail
And catch the winds of destiny
Wherever they drive the boat.
To put meaning in one's life may end in madness,
But life without meaning is the torture
Of restlessness and vague desire—
It is a boat longing for the sea and yet afraid.

—Edgar Lee Masters

On December 14, 2012, after seven years teaching at Sandy Hook Elementary, the world turned upside down.

In trying to find our way forward, I knew we needed to help the children rediscover a sense of control over their lives, and to create strategies to ensure that the tragedy would not come to define us.

Inspiration came one day. People sent everything from Happy Meal parties to teddy bears. You name it, they sent it. I asked my students, "Does anyone know why someone did this for us?" "They wanted to be nice!" I said, "You're absolutely right. And when somebody does something nice for you, you do something nice for someone else. That's the way the world is meant to work."

I told them that we would find a class in need and send them a gift. "We're going to make them feel the way we feel right now: happy." My kids were so excited to know they could do good in the world, be the good in the world, even after such tragedy. And so Classes4Classes was born.

When I was a child, my mother read me "The Road Not Taken." I was captivated by the line, "I took the one less traveled by, and that has made all the difference." These words have guided my belief that children need to know that they hold the keys to their lives.

As teachers, we have the power to inspire our students, to motivate them, and to let them know that no matter what happens, their path is up to them.

—*Kaitlin Roig*
Elementary School Teacher
Newtown, Connecticut

The Road Not Taken

Two roads diverged in a yellow wood,
And sorry I could not travel both
And be one traveler, long I stood
And looked down one as far as I could
To where it bent in the undergrowth;

Then took the other, as just as fair,
And having perhaps the better claim,
Because it was grassy and wanted wear;
Though as for that the passing there
Had worn them really about the same,

And both that morning equally lay
In leaves no step had trodden black.
Oh, I kept the first for another day!
Yet knowing how way leads on to way,
I doubted if I should ever come back.

I shall be telling this with a sigh
Somewhere ages and ages hence:
Two roads diverged in a wood, and I—
I took the one less traveled by,
And that has made all the difference.

—*Robert Frost*

I vividly recall first encountering Rudyard Kipling's "IF" in my sophomore English literature class in Chesterfield, England. After a month of Keats's abstract Romanticism, I was relieved to find something more tangible that connected to my teenage angst and the looming reality that, contrary to my early aspirations, I wasn't destined to be England's next great rugby or cricket superstar. I needed a new road map to guide me past the disappointment of being a sporting genius trapped in the body of a markedly average athlete. Each time I revisited the poem, it reaffirmed a growing belief that there was something to be said for being an "all-rounder," to borrow a cricketing term.

Now, Kipling's poem guides my teaching and coaching as I try to help my students understand that true character is formed out of a multitude of traits and attributes. In a world that stresses the importance of individual excellence, a reminder of the virtues of humility, integrity, modesty, patience, and empathy can provide unexpected solace for youth.

Admittedly, the undertones of Kipling's imperialism are hard to disentangle from his works. Students recognize this, and so they ought. Yet, when taken at face value, Kipling's words can help us "keep our head" as we "meet with Triumph and Disaster."

As a fresh-faced ninth grader so succinctly put it, "I get it, Coach . . . he's saying if I do X, Y, and Z, I'll be doing all right!" It may not be "the Earth," but maybe "doing all right" isn't so bad after all.

—Andy Wood

High School History Teacher and Soccer Coach
Northampton, Massachusetts

IF

If you can keep your head when all about you
   Are losing theirs and blaming it on you,
If you can trust yourself when all men doubt you,
   But make allowance for their doubting too;
If you can wait and not be tired by waiting,
   Or being lied about, don't deal in lies,
Or being hated, don't give way to hating,
   And yet don't look too good, nor talk too wise:

If you can dream—and not make dreams your master
   If you can think—and not make thoughts your aim
If you can meet with Triumph and Disaster
   And treat those two impostors just the same;
If you can bear to hear the truth you've spoken
   Twisted by knaves to make a trap for fools,
Or watch the things you gave your life to, broken,
   And stoop and build 'em up with worn-out tools:

If you can make one heap of all your winnings
   And risk it on one turn of pitch-and-toss,
And lose, and start again at your beginnings
   And never breathe a word about your loss;
If you can force your heart and nerve and sinew
   To serve your turn long after they are gone,
And so hold on when there is nothing in you
   Except the Will which says to them: 'Hold on!'

If you can talk with crowds and keep your virtue,
   Or walk with Kings—nor lose the common touch,
If neither foes nor loving friends can hurt you,
   If all men count with you, but none too much;
If you can fill the unforgiving minute
   With sixty seconds' worth of distance run,
Yours is the Earth and everything that's in it,
   And—which is more—you'll be a Man, my son!

               —*Rudyard Kipling*

Jonathan sat at the back of the classroom. At nine years old, he was already convinced that the world hated him—and the dark energy he put out was not helping.

On the first day of our summer academic enrichment program, he flung his belongings into the coatroom, while his mom stood by nervously and whispered, "He's failing in school, but we hope you'll see his potential."

When I passed out copies of a questionnaire for the students to fill out, Jonathan was already defeated.

"I'm stupid," he said. "I can't write."

I decided this was the last time Jonathan would be wrong in my class.

During our three-week program on the theme "Design Your Own Universe," students each envisioned their own ideal world by drawing pictures, making maps, building models, and telling stories. Although Jonathan struggled with his writing, his *ideas* were brilliant. And when he was free to create in the ways he liked best, he eventually relaxed and even made a few friends. On the last day of the program, Jonathan proudly went first, telling a beautiful fantasy story about a hero who makes his way through an upside-down universe.

Jonathan was a gifted thinker and storyteller, but his self-concept had been warped by a school system that told him to sit down, to be quiet, and that his words and ideas only counted if he could print them neatly.

Loris Malaguzzi's poem reminds me of the courage of students who, like Jonathan, just need the time and space to rediscover the hundred worlds within.

—*Tiffany Poirier*
Elementary School Teacher
Surrey, British Columbia, Canada

No Way. The Hundred is There.

The child
is made of one hundred.
The child has
a hundred languages
a hundred hands
a hundred thoughts
a hundred ways of thinking
of playing, of speaking.
A hundred always a hundred
ways of listening
of marveling, of loving
a hundred joys
for singing and understanding
a hundred worlds
to discover
a hundred worlds
to invent
a hundred worlds
to dream.
The child has
a hundred languages
(and a hundred hundred hundred more)
but they steal ninety-nine.
The school and the culture
separate the head from the body.

They tell the child:
to think without hands
to do without head
to listen and not to speak
to understand without joy
to love and to marvel
only at Easter and Christmas.
They tell the child:
to discover the world already there
and of the hundred
they steal ninety-nine.
They tell the child:
that work and play
reality and fantasy
science and imagination
sky and earth
reason and dream
are things
that do not belong together.

And thus they tell the child
that the hundred is not there.
The child says
No way. The hundred *is* there.

—*Loris Malaguzzi*

As an undergraduate, I gave new meaning to the term *undecided*. Before I settled on my fifth major, I tried music performance, music education, industrial engineering, and creative writing. I was determined not to become an English teacher—like my mother. But destiny was unavoidable. Teaching is a calling. It is an inescapable passion also shared by my grandfather, aunt, and sister.

Like my mother, I have read this poem with middle school students, graduate students, and students of every level in between. The breathless nature of the poem resonates with classroom life and echoes the foreboding sense of time ticking. The knotted, snapped shoelaces, frayed shirts, and clogged bottles evoke the very human nature of learning—messy, recursive, frustrating, and fraught with risk. Somehow the events and people in the poem come together. The poem reveals the moments of power and beauty that emerge when we trust one another and leap into the unknown—the kind of learning that really counts.

The last stanza, which makes me cry every time I read it, captures the contradiction that we as teachers must hold in our minds. As an educator, I have arrived: I understand my craft and can apply my expertise. Yet, I know I will never be ready—not entirely. I must remain idealistic, trusting that my students and I (and maybe a text or two) will embark on a journey whose end may be just out of sight.

So we set off. As long as we're together, we'll be okay.

Ready or not, let's go.

—Julie A. Gorlewski
College Professor of Education
New Paltz, New York

Lessons

"No one is ever ready!"
My father barks the time,
and the clocks race on
as I re-tie my laces
for the third time
and my brother hunts
for his belt in a drawerful
of underwear and frayed shirts
and my mother is undoing
the catch of a dress
too formal or not formal
enough for such an occasion,
and my father is still waiting
and letting us know it
and the laces snap
in my hands where
I knotted a new break
only yesterday, and my brother's
drawer gets stuck half-open
with his best belt
just out of reach,
and my mother's perfume-bomb
won't spray, and all of a sudden
it's so late

we have to rush
out of the house
without finishing any-
thing, and somehow or other
my brother has got hold of a belt
(if not his best) and
my laces will hold (just barely)
for a few more hours, and my mother
looks great in the mirror
and smells like herself up close,
and my father jams the key
in the ignition and *we're off*
to some life-or-death destination

No one is ever ready
is what I learned
on those breathless childhood nights,
before I learned that ends
and means may coincide, in time,
and destinations lose their meaning.
I am still waiting; I have arrived;
I will never be ready.

—*Gerald Jonas*

A few times a year, I play poker with a group of lawyers, business owners, federal government employees, and software developers. Not long ago, one of them turned to me and asked, "So, what's it like to be a public school teacher?"

The question was asked innocently enough, but the emphasis on "public" and the unspoken meaning—"Why would anyone be a public school teacher?"—threw me off balance. I would have loved to have had the wit of poet Taylor Mali and launched into a ferocious comeback worthy of his poem "What Teachers Make."

I didn't.

Instead, I gave a passionate defense of the impact I have on the lives of young people, every single day, and then proceeded to win a few rounds of cards. Still, I could hear Mali's poem ringing in my ear.

I've shared Mali's poem with other educators in many professional development sessions, and I've given the poem as a gift to colleagues. With its defiant tone, the poem becomes a token of solidarity, and I am reminded of a quote from Charlie Parker that I use as the tagline for my blog: "If you don't live it, it won't come out of your horn."[2] The poem resonates with a similar message: as educators, we need to be proud of what we do and boldly confront misconceptions that surround us.

It's almost as important as the work we do each and every day in the classroom.

—Kevin Hodgson
Elementary School Teacher
Southampton, Massachusetts

---

2. R. Reisner, *Bird: The Legend of Charlie Parker* (Boston: Da Capo Press, 1977), 27.

What Teachers Make

He says the problem with teachers is
What's a kid going to learn
from someone who decided his best option in life
was to become a teacher?
He reminds the other dinner guests that it's true
what they say about teachers:
Those who can, do; those who can't, teach.
I decide to bite my tongue instead of his
and resist the temptation to remind the dinner guests
that it's also true what they say about lawyers.
Because we're eating, after all, and this is polite conversation.

I mean, you're a teacher, Taylor.
Be honest. What do you make?

And I wish he hadn't done that—asked me to be honest—
because, you see, I have this policy about honesty and ass-kicking:
if you ask for it, then I have to let you have it.
You want to know what I make?
I make kids work harder than they ever thought they could.
I can make a C+ feel like a Congressional Medal of Honor
and an A– feel like a slap in the face.
How dare you waste my time
with anything less than your very best.
I make kids sit through 40 minutes of study hall
in absolute silence. *No, you may not work in groups.*
No, you may not ask a question.
Why won't I let you go to the bathroom?
Because you're bored.
And you don't really have to go to the bathroom, do you?

I make parents tremble in fear when I call home:
Hi. This is Mr. Mali. I hope I haven't called at a bad time,
I just wanted to talk to you about something your son said today.
To the biggest bully in the grade, he said,
"Leave the kid alone. I still cry sometimes, don't you?
It's no big deal."
And that was the noblest act of courage I have ever seen.
I make parents see their children for who they are
and what they can be.

You want to know what I make? I make kids wonder,
I make them question.
I make them criticize.
I make them apologize and mean it.
I make them write.
I make them read, read, read.
I make them spell *definitely beautiful, definitely beautiful, definitely beautiful*
over and over and over again until they will never misspell
either one of those words again.
I make them show all their work in math
and hide it on their final drafts in English.
I make them understand that if you've got *this*,
then you follow *this*,
and if someone ever tries to judge you
by what you make, you give them *this*.
Here, let me break it down for you, so you know what I say is true:
Teachers make a goddamn difference! Now what about you?

—*Taylor Mali*

Teachable Moments

*T*ime-lapse photography offers us a way to witness the miracle of physical growth in incremental moments. It makes accessible the metamorphosis of a butterfly from egg, to caterpillar, to pupa, to exquisite winged creature. Seeing the gradual unfolding of life clarifies what had been eternally mysterious. Yet, despite our technological wizardry, no machine or lens or evaluation or test can truly capture the precise moment when learning happens. These moments are often enigmatic and ephemeral—yet teachers know them in their bones.

Teachers revel in moments when something "clicks" for a young person, when they discern a student experiencing a fragile and imperceptible pulse of insight, or when they intuit that something has tangibly coalesced for their class as a whole. These teachable moments represent the grail of practice. They indicate a breakthrough, and teachers treasure their arrival.

Although teachers appreciate these artful, often quiet and subtle moments as evidence of the worth of good teaching, this "mode" of knowing and the powerful practice that supports it have been pushed to the margins. The poems and commentaries in this section offer a nuanced view of the complex moment when learning takes place.

The teachers describe how reading poetry provides a low-tech version of time-lapse photography. Poetry captures the single luminous moment. From this moment, we can reflect, savor, and more deeply understand.

Though it happened a year ago, I can still hear that resounding slap when Treveon's foot connected with a red kickball. He booted a low, bouncing pitch, rolled out by a hapless fourth grader, above the play structure, past the flagpole, and down to the street below.

Picture a hundred upturned faces tracking the path of that hurtling red orb as it rose, fell, and then vanished beyond the chain-link fence. Time stopped, birds chirped in hushed tones, even clouds made way. Then a cry went up from the blacktop, and I heard a chorus of children crying out in a perfect "Ooooh." Say it out loud, and you will understand.

Treveon's kick reminded me of transcendent moments in each school day—moments that light up the sky and light me up as well. When even one of my four hundred students steps beyond where he or she thought was possible, I get to go there too—and take one more step in my own unfolding. I can find light, my playground church, every single day and be called into my strength again.

Rainier Maria Rilke's shining words tell me that angels have faces like our own. They walk among us on the gritty scrabble within these school yard fences. He calls on me to revere the power of service and the growth that comes when we don't hold back. In the end, all that I am is all that I ever have to give. I'm good with that.

—*Gregory John*
Principal
Starr King Elementary School
San Francisco, California

All will come again into its strength

All will come again into its strength:
the fields undivided, the waters undammed,
the trees towering and the walls built low.
And in the valleys, people as strong
and varied as the land.

And no churches where God
is imprisoned and lamented
like a trapped and wounded animal.
The houses welcoming all who knock
and a sense of boundless offering
in all relations, and in you and me.

No yearning for an afterlife, no looking beyond,
no belittling of death,
but only longing for what belongs to us
and serving earth, lest we remain unused.

—*Rainier Maria Rilke*

They are so young. Standing in front of a classroom of twenty-seven ardent faces, young bodies clothed in baggy sweatshirts and short shorts, accessorized with neon hair and black bracelets, hunched over their journals, writing—you smile knowingly, thinking, *They are so young*.

Holding that view makes it simpler, it's true, to grade that essay quickly, to lift your insights over theirs, to sigh at the exclamation points mixed with question marks at the end of every other sentence. To roll your eyes at the drama. To be grateful, for them, that as they mature, most of that clackity-clacking will even out. That they will find themselves, ten years from now on some street corner, finally recognizing what it is to be alive.

You're standing in front of your English class, thinking this, when you open a book of poems and land on Richard Wilbur's "The Writer." The speaker is listening to his daughter clackity-clacking on a typewriter, writing a story. *She is young*, he thinks, and smiles.

You understand, and smile, too.

But it turns out that you only think you do—understand—or more accurately, that you used to. Because the rest of Wilbur's poem takes you back to yourself, a young girl under a maple tree, pen in hand, who knew regardless of her age what it was to be alive. And then you look back to your students, each of them, who—underneath their baggy clothes and eyeliner—are grappling with words as old as the earth, and getting them right.

—*Emily Brisse*
High School English Teacher
Watertown, Minnesota

The Writer

In her room at the prow of the house
Where light breaks, and the windows are tossed with linden,
My daughter is writing a story.

I pause in the stairwell, hearing
From her shut door a commotion of typewriter-keys
Like a chain hauled over a gunwale.

Young as she is, the stuff
Of her life is a great cargo, and some of it heavy:
I wish her a lucky passage.

But now it is she who pauses,
As if to reject my thought and its easy figure.
A stillness greatens, in which

The whole house seems to be thinking,
And then she is at it again with a bunched clamor
Of strokes, and again is silent.

I remember the dazed starling
Which was trapped in that very room, two years ago;
How we stole in, lifted a sash

And retreated, not to affright it;
And how for a helpless hour, through the crack of the door,
We watched the sleek, wild, dark

And iridescent creature
Batter against the brilliance, drop like a glove
To the hard floor, or the desk-top,

And wait then, humped and bloody,
For the wits to try it again; and how our spirits
Rose when, suddenly sure,

It lifted off from a chair-back,
Beating a smooth course for the right window
And clearing the sill of the world.

It is always a matter, my darling,
Of life or death, as I had forgotten. I wish
What I wished you before, but harder.

—*Richard Wilbur*

During my first year teaching at a small Quaker school, I assigned "The Waking" by Theodore Roethke to a class of seniors. My intention was to discuss it and use it to analyze the form of the villanelle, but I was soon struck by its applicability to this special moment in my students' lives.

Seniors occupy a liminal period. As they move closer to graduation it becomes a time of great import and fear. It can be difficult for students, particularly anxious ones, to remember that we "learn by going where we have to go."

Over the many years that I have taught seniors, I have watched them, as they approach graduation, become increasingly unnerved. Some push friends away because they are preparing for separation. Some neglect responsibilities because they are unable to stay in the present moment. Others shut down, afraid of the leap to college and leaving the familiar behind.

"The Waking" reminds me that this sort of apprehension is natural and, in fact, can be centering: "This shaking keeps me steady." Roethke's line is oxymoronic, yes, but often the messages graduating students hear are equally contradictory—they are told simultaneously to treasure every waning moment while turning boldly toward the future. Roethke writes, "What falls away is always. And is near." Eventually, the experience of high school, the day-to-day, falls away, but the transformative moments are always near, following us as we go forth.

—Nora Landon

High School English Teacher
Philadelphia, Pennsylvania

The Waking

I wake to sleep, and take my waking slow.
I feel my fate in what I cannot fear.
I learn by going where I have to go.

We think by feeling. What is there to know?
I hear my being dance from ear to ear.
I wake to sleep, and take my waking slow.

Of those so close beside me, which are you?
God bless the Ground! I shall walk softly there,
And learn by going where I have to go.

Light takes the Tree; but who can tell us how?
The lowly worm climbs up a winding stair;
I wake to sleep, and take my waking slow.

Great Nature has another thing to do
To you and me; so take the lively air,
And, lovely, learn by going where to go.

This shaking keeps me steady. I should know.
What falls away is always. And is near.
I wake to sleep, and take my waking slow.
I learn by going where I have to go.

—*Theodore Roethke*

I love Emily Dickinson because her life and her writing were such a contrast. From what all the world could see, she was shy and quiet, but her writing shows her passionate soul. She was not an outwardly joyful person, but inside she was a fighter and an adventurer and a person who saw deeply the joy of life. This poem shows her courageous soul that wanted to live and risk and understood that she would fail many times, and so what? Whatever possibility of pain is worth the possibility of joy.

That's what I wanted to teach my sixth graders. Life is beautiful with all its dangers and sadness. It's not perfect, and if it were perfect, it would be boring. It is simply worth living and living with all your heart. Aspire. Risk. Don't be afraid of failure, be terrified of not trying.

Dickinson speaks to my professional struggles. I ran for Congress and lost. But the loss opened up other opportunities, and I am now vice president of the National Education Association, which represents over three million passionate educators. Dickinson speaks to my personal struggles. I was the Teacher of the Year, yet I struggled to help my own son fight his addiction. I organized to empower educators, yet I struggled to help my own husband fight his lifelong depression.

Life, in victory, is sweet, of course. But life, in defeat, is still life. *Vale la pena.* It is worth any pain to experience the joy of simply living.

—*Lily Eskelsen García*
Vice President
National Education Association
Washington, DC

'Tis so much joy! 'Tis so much joy!
If I should fail, what poverty!
And yet, as poor as I,
Have ventured all opon a throw!
Have gained! Yes! Hesitated so–
This side the Victory!

Life is but life! And Death, but Death!
Bliss is but Bliss, and Breath but Breath!
And if indeed I fail,
At least, to know the worst, is sweet!
Defeat means nothing *but* Defeat,
No drearier, can befall!

And if I gain! Oh Gun at sea,
Oh Bells, that in the steeples be!
At first, repeat it slow!
For Heaven is a different thing,
Conjectured, and waked sudden in–
And might extinguish me!

—*Emily Dickinson*

At the age of fifty-nine, after a thirty-year career as a freelance writer and video producer, I asked myself: *What is the most important work I could do before retiring?* The answer appeared to me with irrefutable clarity: teach the children most at risk.

I am now approaching the end of my first year with the Urban Teacher Center. I teach second grade while simultaneously pursuing my teacher's license and graduate degree. It is daunting and exhausting to start anew. Every day, I am humbled by how little I know, how much I lack in teaching experience, how badly I fumble the basics of classroom management. Pushing me through the challenges is my passion to share with my students an appreciation for the beauty, diversity, and ridiculousness of life on Earth.

My sense of reverence for this "DNA experiment station" was clarified nearly twenty years ago when I came across Paul Boswell's "This Splendid Speck" in the *Washington Post*. The poem celebrates Earth's unique vibrancy among the planets of our solar system. Only on this one "blue and white exception" have single-celled organisms evolved into water lilies, whales, and Gershwin. And, I would add, into Common Core State Standards and second graders who every day surprise me with their insights and their needs. Some of them have already seen how life can be "lethal or lucky." Still they express love, laughter, and wonder.

My second graders are not altogether ready for all of what infuses Boswell's poem. Nevertheless, I can and do teach them about peacocks, anchovies, the moon . . . and poetry.

—Christine Intagliata
Elementary School Teaching Resident
Washington, DC

This Splendid Speck

There are no peacocks on Venus,
No oak trees or water lilies on Jupiter,
No squirrels or whales or figs on Mercury,
No anchovies on the moon;

And inside the rings of Saturn
There is no species that makes poems
And Intercontinental missiles.

Eight wasted planets,
Several dozen wasted moons.

In all the Sun's half-lighted entourage
One unbelievable blue and white exception,
This breeding, feeding, bleeding,
Cloud-peekaboo Earth,
Is not dead as a diamond.

This splendid speck,
This DNA experiment station,
Where life seems, somehow,
To have designed or assembled itself;
Where Chance and Choice
Play at survival and extinction;

Where molecules beget molecules,
And mistakes in the begetting
May be inconsequential,
Or lethal or lucky;
Where life everywhere eats life
And reproduction usually outpaces cannibalism;

This bloody paradise
Where, under the Northern lights,
Sitting choirs of white wolves
Howl across the firmament
Their chill *Te Deums*.
Where, in lower latitudes, matter more articulate
Gets a chance at consciousness
And invents *The Messiah*, or *The Marseillaise*,
The Ride of the Valkyries, or *The Rhapsody in Blue*.

This great blue pilgrim gyroscope,
Warmer than Mars, cooler than Venus,
Old turner of temperature nights and days,
This best of all reachable worlds,

This blessed speck.

—*Paul Boswell*

As educators, we never really know the power and effect of our words or actions. Just as Miss Murphy's offhand comment about the potential end of the world triggered Stanley Kunitz's narrator's nighttime adventure on his roof, the impact of the words and gestures of those of us who work with youth is unknown and immeasurable, no matter how many evaluation tools we devise to assess them. All of our anecdotal experiences amount to a data set impossible to analyze or truly comprehend.

As the program director for Harlem RBI—a youth development organization where youth play baseball and softball to learn, grow, and realize their dreams—I can see that the needs of the youth are great. Yet often we have only an inkling of the unspoken and unknown adversities they endure outside of our schools, programs, workshops, or practices.

On the field and in our programs, the opportunities for impact are nearly boundless: a coach's figurative or literal pat on the back, a counselor's home visit, or a mentor's smile and look of acknowledgment. These many small signs provide youth with inspiration, love, and confidence that can influence them for a lifetime.

This poem brings this point home and gets me to take the time to talk with these kids, to stay a few hours later than usual to get some program or training right, to make that additional phone call to a family, or to seize an opportunity to help a youth or inspire a program staff member.

—Rob Maitra
Director of Programs
Harlem RBI
New York, New York

Halley's Comet

Miss Murphy in first grade
wrote its name in chalk
across the board and told us
it was roaring down the stormtracks
of the Milky Way at frightful speed
and if it wandered off its course
and smashed into the earth
there'd be no school tomorrow.
A red-bearded preacher from the hills
with a wild look in his eyes
stood in the public square
at the playground's edge
proclaiming he was sent by God
to save every one of us,
even the little children.
"Repent, ye sinners!" he shouted,
waving his hand-lettered sign.
At supper I felt sad to think
that it was probably
the last meal I'd share
with my mother and my sisters;
but I felt excited too
and scarcely touched my plate.

So mother scolded me
and sent me early to my room.
The whole family's asleep
except for me. They never heard me steal
into the stairwell hall and climb
the ladder to the fresh night air.
Look for me, Father, on the roof
of the red brick building
at the foot of Green Street—
that's where we live, you know, on the top floor.
I'm the boy in the white flannel gown
sprawled on this coarse gravel bed
searching the starry sky,
waiting for the world to end.

—*Stanley Kunitz*

Ever since my first day of teaching, I've displayed this poem in a simple frame on my desk. I try to live my life by its compelling call to action.

One day, I shared the poem with my seventh graders. A stirring discussion ensued. We talked about how it felt to help someone in need or perform random good deeds. I gave my students one simple assignment: "Do something nice for someone."

The next day, they were eager to talk about their good deeds: helping an elderly grandparent, assisting a sibling with homework, doing extra chores around the house.

A week later, I received a letter from the mother of one of my students. She described how she had been at her wits' end and had been thinking of sending her son, Thomas, to live with his father even though he lived far away from Thomas's familiar surroundings and friends. But then Thomas came home and offered to help with dinner. After a bit, he told her about his homework assignment. She had hugged him, so grateful for his kind gesture. "Not only did he help with dinner, but he did the dishes afterward! Ever since, he's like a different kid—so much nicer, so much more helpful. I can't stop hugging him!"

A beautiful poem led to a homework assignment, which led to a child's good deed, which led to his mother's hugs (desperately needed), which initiated the start of a healthier relationship between mother and child. The poem still sits on my desk, but Thomas etched it on my heart.

—*Annette Breaux*

Author, Speaker, and Educator
Houma, Louisiana

If I can stop one Heart from breaking
I shall not live in vain
If I can ease one Life the Aching
Or cool one Pain

Or help one fainting Robin
Unto his Nest again
I shall not live in vain.

—*Emily Dickinson*

I work with students who consistently fail at this process we call school. They live a nightmare and find little solace for their wounded psyches. They've settled into a pattern of disenchantment, of "weight deadened on their shoulders." I try to share with them the geography of possibility and beauty and warmth that lies within them. I encourage them to search for what delights and animates them.

Alexander came to the Maine Academy of Natural Sciences—a high school focused on farming, forestry, sustainability, and alternative energy—with few credits and little sense of achievement. He had moved from school to school, had a pattern of rarely finishing anything, and refused to do things that did not move him. Yet he bloomed at the Academy—helping to create community through the development of his Orchard Park, a park on our campus devoted to growing perennial fruits complete with walkways and benches. To one degree or another, we have all been touched by Alexander's vision and pulled into it.

John O'Donohue's poem is a blessing. It juxtaposes the darkness we experience with the joys that patiently wait for us to see them. It shows us that darkness can be transformed into "the clarity of light" through the act of heartfelt creativity and loving compassion.

"Beannacht" embodies my wish that those I work with and teach will find themselves safe and loved and capable of moving beyond the dark shores of their past into a vibrant and rich present. All journeying students deserve the "protection of the ancestors," now and in years to come.

—*Emanuel Pariser*

Co-founder and Director of Instruction
Maine Academy of Natural Sciences
Hinckley, Maine

Beannacht

On the day when
the weight deadens
on your shoulders
and you stumble,
may the clay dance
to balance you.

And when your eyes
freeze behind
the grey window
and the ghost of loss
gets in to you,
may a flock of colours,
indigo, red, green
and azure blue
come to awaken in you
a meadow of delight.

When the canvas frays
in the currach of thought
and a stain of ocean
blackens beneath you,
may there come across the waters
a path of yellow moonlight
to bring you safely home.

May the nourishment of the earth be yours,
may the clarity of light be yours,
may the fluency of the ocean be yours,
may the protection of the ancestors be yours.

And so may a slow
wind work these words
of love around you,
an invisible cloak
to mind your life.

—*John O'Donohue*

The best part of being a school superintendent was visiting elementary class-rooms, where the range of emotions associated with learning were transparent—confusion, engagement, frustration, and pride. Most expressive are first-grade classrooms, where letters become words and words become meaning—and each synaptic connection comes with the release of unadulterated joy.

By the intermediate grades, emotions are more contained, but students still get that look when they are totally engrossed—when you can see the wheels turning, and the wry smile that comes when the lightbulbs go off.

D. H. Lawrence learned firsthand about the joys and frustrations of teaching in a school for boys. "The Best of School" captures the "glad thrill" of watching the puzzled look turn to the satisfaction of learning. And, "Having found what he wanted," Lawrence reflected, "their thrills are mine."

These days I spend my time finding, describing, and supporting new learning environments that are challenging and supportive—high tech and high touch. We have a chance to create engaging and inspiring schools that produce more best days for students and teachers—schools where students are motivated by powerful learning experiences; schools where teachers work in collaborative teams with powerful tools; schools where students and teachers feel respected, inspired, and supported.

This poem is my favorite description of the job of watching students "darting away with discovery" and of the subtle satisfaction of watching them find the "thrills" that are "the best of school."

—*Tom Vander Ark*
CEO
Getting Smart
Tacoma, Washington

The Best of School

The blinds are drawn because of the sun,
And the boys and the room in colourless gloom
Of underwater float: bright ripples run
Across the walls as the blinds are blown
To let the sunlight in; and I,
As I sit on the shores of the class, alone,
Watch the boys in their summer blouses
As they write, their round heads busily bowed:
And one after another rouses
His face to look at me,
To ponder very quietly,
As seeing, he does not see.

And then he turns again, with a little, glad
Thrill of his work he turns again from me,
Having found what he wanted, having got what was
     to be had.

And very sweet it is, while the sunlight waves
In the ripening morning, to sit alone with the class
And feel the stream of awakening ripple and pass
From me to the boys, whose brightening souls it laves
For this little hour.

This morning, sweet it is
To feel the lads' looks light on me,
Then back in a swift, bright flutter to work;
Each one darting away with his
Discovery, like birds that steal and flee.

Touch after touch I feel on me
As their eyes glance at me for the grain
Of rigour they taste delightedly.

As tendrils reach out yearningly,
Slowly rotate till they touch the tree
That they cleave unto, and up which they climb
Up to their lives—so they to me.

I feel them cling and cleave to me
As vines going eagerly up; they twine
My life with other leaves, my time
Is hidden in theirs, their thrills are mine.

—D. H. Lawrence

Beauty in the Ordinary

*G*ood teachers are steadfast—that is, they stand firm, faithful, and resolute. They are methodical and systematic, yet they do their work in highly fluid and complex environments. Teachers make hundreds of decisions a day: responding to students, asking questions, and adjudicating conflict. Teaching requires the capacity to work a plan, but also the agility to improvise.

To keep their balance, good teachers put in place powerful routines that support learning and the building of community. These procedures may not be glamorous, but they function as the linchpin of life in a classroom. Much as the stonemason values the wedge-shaped keystone that serves as the apex on an arch and locks the stones into position, allowing it to bear weight, teachers appreciate the significance of creating stability and predictability within the multidimensionality of the classroom.

The teachers in this section understand the importance of minding the small but indispensable routines that constitute their work. The work of good teaching is quiet, hidden, and often immeasurably subtle. The ordinary rhythms of teaching have an aesthetic beauty and a quality of craftsmanship that emerge in the stories teachers share.

Sometimes I dream of doing something great, like writing a book or earning another degree. Although those would be wonderful goals and accomplishments, Fernando Pessoa's poem reminds me that to truly be great, I need to be like the moon—dependable and wholly present.

It's just as important, if not more so, to shine in the small, daily tasks of life and work. Consistently encouraging students, preparing engaging lessons and activities, and maintaining open communication with parents are hallmarks of being a good teacher, even though these aspects of my work may not garner much attention or fanfare.

I have never been able to rouse myself to get excited about writing report cards, but it's a necessary and important part of the job. So I've spent countless hours "hunkered down" at my desk, agonizing over each word, even though I suspect that sometimes the comments may be skimmed over in a rush to look at the grades or scores. There is nothing glamorous or earth-shattering about this task. However, I do take pride in completing the reports accurately, providing encouraging comments and helpful recommendations. I offer my observations of the student and knowledge about teaching and learning, and know I have done my best to help a child discover the miracle of reading.

Do I give all tasks the kind of focus and attention they deserve? No, it's a tall order. I often read this poem to remember that I can be great by giving the best of myself in all things.

—Vicki Den Ouden
Elementary School Reading Intervention Teacher
Kelowna, British Columbia, Canada

To Be Great, Be Entire

To be great, be entire:
Of what is yours nothing
exaggerate or exclude
Be whole in each thing. Put all that you are
Into the least you do
Like that on each place the whole moon
Shines for she lives aloft.

—*Fernando Pessoa*

I first came across this poem after a long, defeating Wednesday. I teach in the Khartoum International Community School in Sudan, where the spectrum of perspectives can be challenging. Like teachers anywhere, I simply cannot win all the battles with time, other adults, germs, worries, and the scorching sun.

I know I will never be spectacular in the way that I yearn to be. I can, however, be famous to my students, like "the river is famous to the fish." I can teach them how to listen to each other, so they can take turns chasing the threads of their beautiful minds. I can laugh with them, every day. I can show them how I fall and stand again, so I can learn. I can stop them, to demand better of them, before they carry on. I can remember that working for them is the best that I can be.

Naomi Shihab Nye's poem is about the relativity of importance and, within that, the roles that people play. I appreciate her choice of a buttonhole and a pulley to close the poem, because of the reliability and the solidity they represent. Their fame lies in their ubiquity and steadfastness.

I love that point in the year when my students start their morning meeting before I enter the classroom. I love when I stand unnoticed while they are deep in discussion, using the pathways I showed them. I am famous because I am unseen but assumed, unsought but present in their hearts and their words.

—*Safaa Abdel-Magid*
Elementary School Teacher
Khartoum, The Sudan

Famous

The river is famous to the fish.

The loud voice is famous to silence,
which knew it would inherit the earth
before anybody said so.

The cat sleeping on the fence is famous to the birds
watching him from the birdhouse.

The tear is famous, briefly, to the cheek.

The idea you carry close to your bosom
is famous to your bosom.

The boot is famous to the earth,
more famous than the dress shoe,
which is famous only to floors.

The bent photograph is famous to the one who carries it
and not at all famous to the one who is pictured.

I want to be famous to shuffling men
who smile while crossing streets,
sticky children in grocery lines,
famous as the one who smiled back.

I want to be famous in the way a pulley is famous,
or a buttonhole, not because it did anything spectacular,
but because it never forgot what it could do.

—Naomi Shihab Nye

Most days, teaching can feel like ironing, like busywork that must be done well enough to go unmentioned. We take attendance, issue hall passes, and write letters of recommendation. Even our love of the subject and the students is often seen, at least on the outside, as just subjects to be mastered, lessons to be covered, and students to be taught and passed to the next grade. And because everyone has been to school, it all seems ordinary unless a movie director romanticizes the experience, or things go poorly. The rest seems unremarkable.

What I want to say is that there is also beauty in this routine. I've had my own share of little triumphs to sustain me, but I just can't hold my breath from shining moment to shining moment. I wouldn't have made it this far in teaching without also loving the ironing, the quiet pleasure of huddling over a draft with a student to make the writing sing.

In his poem, Pablo Neruda restores a pile of damp garments to purity in the space of thirteen lines, and every time I read it, I wonder: *Is it possible to approach my teaching from a position of praise and questioning, just as Neruda approached the world?* Our teaching and all that makes it familiar and viable aren't mere happenstance; our hands have labored together to make this reality. The best we can do is keep them "moving, moving," because on the luckiest and most ordinary of days, we are "creating the world."

—*Cindy O'Donnell-Allen*

College Professor and Director
Colorado State University Writing Project
Fort Collins, Colorado

In Praise of Ironing

Poetry is pure white.
It emerges from water covered with drops,
is wrinkled, all in a heap.
It has to be spread out, the skin of this planet,
has to be ironed out, the sea's whiteness;
and the hands keep moving, moving,
the holy surfaces are smoothed out,
and that is how things are accomplished.
Every day, hands are creating the world,
fire is married to steel,
and canvas, linen, and cotton come back
from the skirmishings of the laundries,
and out of light a dove is born—
pure innocence returns out of the swirl.

—Pablo Neruda

At the beginning of each school year, I step into the first classroom to a kind of déjà vu. The students are different, yet despite their changed faces I seem to have stepped into this classroom many times before. Generations of students pass through our classes and leave us, bearing the marks of our humanity, while we remain behind. It is this feeling of stillness (immobility highlighted by motion) that Louise Glück's poem captures so well.

My students are almost all from the Inland Empire of California—that sea of suburbs stretching east from Los Angeles to San Bernardino. In the main, they come from immigrant families and have practical goals: to hold a job, to own a car, to support parents and siblings. Sometimes they come back to tell their story. Last year, a twenty-four-year-old former student invited me for a coffee and told me that his dad had left and he was now the sole wage earner. He had just bought a house for his mom and sisters.

My students face real issues. And here is where the love that filters through this poem is meaningful to me. An aubade is a love poem at dawn. In Glück's hands, though, love has less to do with yearning than it does with discovering one's humanity in the sense of stillness accentuated by a kind of movement that never stops.

—Kent Dickson

College Professor of Spanish and Latin American Literature
Pomona, California

Aubade

There was one summer
that returned many times over
there was one flower unfurling
taking many forms

Crimson of the monarda, pale gold of the late roses

There was one love
There was one love, there were many nights

Smell of the mock orange tree
Corridors of jasmine and lilies
Still the wind blew

There were many winters but I closed my eyes
The cold air white with dissolved wings

There was one garden when the snow melted
Azure and white; I couldn't tell
my solitude from love—

There was one love; he had many voices
There was one dawn; sometimes
we watched it together

I was here
I was here

There was one summer returning over and over
there was one dawn
I grew old watching

—Louise Glück

My mother, Barbara Raskin, was a novelist, a journalist, an English professor, and a writer's writer, and when she died in 1999, there was only one poem that gave me any solace at all: W. H. Auden's "In Memory of W. B. Yeats." The key passage for me was:

> Time that is intolerant
> Of the brave and innocent,
> And indifferent in a week
> To a beautiful physique,
>
> Worships language and forgives
> Everyone by whom it lives;

The consolations of this poem for people grieving the loss of a writer are plain. It assures us that the ruthless executioner of all living beings—time—is in love with language and will be gentle with people who have lived by the magic and music of words. None of us can escape death, but language may make us immortal—or at least imperishable in the hearts and minds of others.

As a teacher, I have also come to think of this poem as a touchstone in the classroom. Outside of the classroom, we live by laws and power, wealth and property, inequality and injustice, all the hard realities that life so methodically teaches us on our own. In the classroom, there is a chance, just a chance, that together we will live by the rules of language, which are universal, and explore the possibilities of education, which are infinite and boundless. Through language we might find a little more justice, a little more freedom, and a lot more understanding of the world.

—Jamie Raskin
College Professor of Constitutional Law and Maryland State Senator
Takoma Park, Maryland

From "In Memory of W. B. Yeats"

He disappeared in the dead of winter:
The brooks were frozen, the airports almost deserted,
The snow disfigured the public statues;
The mercury sank in the mouth of the dying day.
O all the instruments agree
The day of his death was a dark cold day.

Far from his illness
The wolves ran on through the evergreen forests,
The peasant river was untempted by the fashionable quays;
By mourning tongues
The death of the poet was kept from his poems. . .

Earth, receive an honoured guest;
William Yeats is laid to rest:
Let the Irish vessel lie
Emptied of its poetry.

Time that is intolerant
Of the brave and the innocent,
And indifferent in a week
To a beautiful physique,

Worships language and forgives
Everyone by whom it lives;
Pardons cowardice, conceit,
Lays its honours at their feet.

Time that with this strange excuse
Pardoned Kipling and his views,

And will pardon Paul Claudel,
Pardons him for writing well.

In the nightmare of the dark
All the dogs of Europe bark,
And the living nations wait,
Each sequestered in its hate;

Intellectual disgrace
Stares from every human face,
And the seas of pity lie
Locked and frozen in each eye.

Follow, poet, follow right
To the bottom of the night,
With your unconstraining voice
Still persuade us to rejoice;

With the farming of a verse
Make a vineyard of the curse,
Sing of human unsuccess
In a rapture of distress;

In the deserts of the heart
Let the healing fountain start,
In the prison of his days
Teach the free man how to praise.

—*W. H. Auden*

The combat boots I wear almost every day communicate a subtle pride in my 2009 deployment to Afghanistan, and they also signify safety, a familiar talisman for my ravaged soul to clutch when some benign element of daily life pushes me toward memory.

The boots help other vets size me up and feel at home. My boots tell them and other attentive students where I've been. Literature can be like my boots—a safe way of traversing dangerous territory and, when wrapped around us as a second skin, proof that what we have chosen to read has shaped the way we choose to live. In "Dedication," Czeslaw Milosz asks, "What is poetry which does not save / Nations or people?" That's a high bar but one I am relentless in trying to reach.

I enjoy teaching historical context, literary form, and linguistic features, but I know they don't have much life-changing value until the class starts out on the right foot of human accountability, of reading as a soul-shaping act.

That's why sometimes I start a class with an anecdote about myself. I've learned that in revealing to students why Walt Whitman's "The Wound-Dresser" recalls my deployment to Afghanistan or how Edward Taylor's "Upon Wedlock, and Death of Children" stirs grief of my own, I become vulnerable. Human. Sometimes a devil. Sometimes a sage. Stephen Crane inspires me to show all sides of myself, knowing that even—or especially—when I'm exposed as a devil students might deride, I still have something to teach.

—*Liam Corley*
College Professor of English
Pomona, California

LVIII

The sage lectured brilliantly.
Before him, two images:
"Now this one is a devil,
And this one is me."
He turned away.
Then a cunning pupil
Changed the positions.
Turned the sage again:
"Now this one is a devil,
And this one is me."
The pupils sat, all grinning,
And rejoiced in the game.
But the sage was a sage.

—*Stephen Crane*

Haily has been my student for three years. She is a beautiful, smart girl with a pain-filled life. Her tough exterior, with her piercings, sailor's mouth, and harrowing war stories, is designed to keep people at bay. When she begins to pull away her mask and open up and share her stories, the exposure becomes too bright; she retreats. She skips class or becomes distant, even cruel.

There are times when I want to pull my feet out of this relationship mire, when the density of the "swamp" seems too difficult to cross. But we keep trudging through the "peerless mud." We are both learning that without the willingness to just show up—even when it feels excruciatingly vulnerable and hard—we can't grow.

Haily, like so many other students with whom I work, reminds me that creating meaningful relationships, the groundwork of education, requires us to enter the "dark burred faintly belching bogs." Mary Oliver's poem encourages me to press on. I read it often, especially when I want to give up and simply pass out worksheets that fence off the swamp and deter any opportunities for engagement and interaction.

Despite swamps of addiction, homelessness, and abuse, Haily will graduate this year. She is budding and branching out to create her own "palace of leaves." I thank Oliver for putting into such luscious words my belief that the struggle in teaching just may result in the "dry stick given one more chance," for something wonderful to take root.

—*Maureen Geraghty*
High School Language Arts Teacher
Portland, Oregon

Crossing the Swamp

Here is the endless
   wet thick
      cosmos, the center
         of everything—the nugget
of dense sap, branching
   vines, the dark burred
      faintly belching
         bogs. Here
is *swamp*, here
   is struggle,
      closure—
         pathless, seamless,
peerless mud. My bones
   knock together at the pale
      joints, trying
         for foothold, fingerhold,
mindhold over
   such slick crossings, deep
      hipholes, hummocks
         that sink silently
into the black, slack
   earthsoup. I feel
      not wet so much as
         painted and glittered

with the fat grassy
   mires, the rich
      and succulent marrows
         of earth—a poor
dry stick given
   one more chance by the whims
      of swamp water—a bough
         that still, after all these years,
could take root,
   sprout, branch out, bud—
      make of its life a breathing
         palace of leaves.

—Mary Oliver

I teach to classrooms of returning war veterans, of older students displaced from their original careers, of high school graduates concerned about debt who attend college close to home. Coming to campus is work in and of itself, and the atmosphere can be heavy with the pressure and expectation of work to come. "What Work Is" is the poem that allows us to meet each other in a common reality. We all know, or think we know, what work is; we can even begin to name how we think it defines us personally, culturally. The poem resonates with the lived tension between dissatisfaction and longing, of the necessity of waiting for what might not arrive. Reading "What Work Is" together allows us to acknowledge that reality, while asking our attention to return to what matters.

Reading the poem also is a solace for me as a professor. Reports and assessments, legislative mandates, the host of demands of teaching at a state institution can make it hard to give way to moments of singing Wagner, or reading poetry, or connecting with whatever it is I love most about teaching.

I believe it is good practice to share that solace with my students. We do come to school to work. Yet the hardest thing isn't all the tasks or the days of waiting; it is opening not only to who and what we love but that we love, and offering that recognition to each other.

—Holly Masturzo

College Professor of Humanities and English
Jacksonville, Florida

What Work Is

We stand in the rain in a long line
waiting at Ford Highland Park. For work.
You know what work is—if you're
old enough to read this you know what
work is, although you may not do it.
Forget you. This is about waiting,
shifting from one foot to another.
Feeling the light rain falling like mist
into your hair, blurring your vision
until you think you see your own brother
ahead of you, maybe ten places.
You rub your glasses with your fingers,
and of course it's someone else's brother,
narrower across the shoulders than
yours but with the same sad slouch, the grin
that does not hide the stubbornness,
the sad refusal to give in to
rain, to the hours of wasted waiting,
to the knowledge that somewhere ahead
a man is waiting who will say, "No,
we're not hiring today," for any
reason he wants. You love your brother,
now suddenly you can hardly stand
the love flooding you for your brother,
who's not beside you or behind or
ahead because he's home trying to
sleep off a miserable night shift

at Cadillac so he can get up
before noon to study his German.
Works eight hours a night so he can sing
Wagner, the opera you hate most,
the worst music ever invented.
How long has it been since you told him
you loved him, held his wide shoulders,
opened your eyes wide and said those words,
and maybe kissed his cheek? You've never
done something so simple, so obvious,
not because you're too young or too dumb,
not because you're jealous or even mean
or incapable of crying in
the presence of another man, no,
just because you don't know what work is.

—*Philip Levine*

Single phrases loop themselves in my mind, relentless soundtracks playing until the phrase's demand is addressed. Lately the looping line is this: "have you reckon'd the earth much?"

Have I? Have I reckoned? My students find literature simultaneously liberating and isolating: Have I reckoned enough to create the place within literature where they understand how necessary they are to it? Our earth is dying; students stand paralyzed by the enormity of the task but willing to try. Have we reckoned? The asking matters. To reckon is to claim responsibility for the quality of the encounter. The student offering a late paper hides her pregnancy. The one falling asleep has a father hooked to a drip bag. The one who asks me, respectfully, to fuck off for noticing her black eye and broken tooth calls years later to say she's sorry. That she was exhausted from always having to be sorry. Have I reckoned?

A dozen times a day, Walt Whitman asks me: "Have you reckon'd . . . ?" The question is always urgent, always human. The answer is never complete.

My students and I have been known to go outside in the pollen-heavy air of spring. From opposite sides of a giant field, we shout lines from "Song of Myself" to each other. I want my students to experience his sprawling, operatic lines; to embody wide-open declarative statements full of giant humanity and grace; to experience what it is to utter a love of the sensory; to shape words of witnessing and acceptance with the tongue and taste how they reside.

—*Jennifer Boyden*
Creative Writing Teacher and Writer
Milton-Freewater, Oregon

Section II from 'Song of Myself'

The smoke of my own breath,
Echoes, ripples, buzz'd whispers, love-root, silk-thread, crotch and
 vine,
My respiration and inspiration, the beating of my heart, the passing
 of blood and air through my lungs,
The sniff of green leaves and dry leaves, and of the shore and
 dark-color'd sea-rocks, and of hay in the barn,
The sound of the belch'd words of my voice loos'd to the eddies of
 the wind,
A few light kisses, a few embraces, a reaching around of arms,
The play of shine and shade on the trees as the supple boughs wag,
The delight alone or in the rush of the streets, or along the fields
 and hill-sides,
The feeling of health, the full-noon trill, the song of me rising from
 bed and meeting the sun.

Have you reckon'd a thousand acres much? have you reckon'd
 the earth much?
Have you practis'd so long to learn to read?
Have you felt so proud to get at the meaning of poems?

Stop this day and night with me and you shall possess the origin
 of all poems,
You shall possess the good of the earth and sun, (there are millions
 of suns left,)
You shall no longer take things at second or third hand, nor look
 through the eyes of the dead, nor feed on the spectres in books,
You shall not look through my eyes either, nor take things from me,
You shall listen to all sides and filter them from your self.

—*Walt Whitman*

Enduring Impact

So much of teaching happens heart-to-heart and face-to-face. Schools are places of high and complex emotion. In classrooms, hallways, and lunchrooms, students and teachers engage each other with their intellects, but also with their feelings, sensitivities, backgrounds, and behaviors.

The poems and commentaries in this section contend with this moral realm and the intense emotional labor expended by teachers in the face-to-face and heart-to-heart encounters of their work. They describe how engaging in the relational work of teaching necessitates putting one's own self on the line. They express how when one stands ready to engage with students and colleagues around hope, fear, aspiration, and purpose, one stands exposed and vulnerable.

Yet it is through this work of seeking out true and genuine connections with students that teachers experience a particularly powerful and enduring reward of teaching. "A teacher affects eternity; he can never tell where his influence stops" is a common inscription on mugs and cards that teachers receive at the end of the year. It's a beguiling message for teachers because it promises that somewhere or sometime in the future a student's behavior, character, or decisions will be shaped by an event or occurrence that transpired in the classroom.

I started teaching one cold January at an inner-city Native American school. I was the third teacher for my students that year. The first weeks were a constant test of whether I could keep all of my students relatively quiet and in the same room.

But the day my grandfather died, there was silence. My students, who had worked as a cohesive team to continually test my limits, now bowed their heads in earnest empathy. "Stop that! Be quiet! Her grandpa just died," they whispered loudly.

These teenagers understood loss. Many had lost immediate family members, often in violent ways. Through loss they could connect with me, could begin to see me as human. It often seems easier to connect with another's suffering than with another's happiness. These sorrowful experiences transform us into empathic people.

My students taught me that when I can be authentic in the classroom, I give them permission to do the same. My vulnerability opens the door for them to believe that I might be not just human, but a human with the capacity for compassion.

I later tattooed on my leg, "Before you know kindness as the deepest thing inside, you must know sorrow as the other deepest thing." It is a constant reminder for me to be authentic about my own sorrow and struggles to myself and to my students. It is a reminder to honor and make space for the sorrow my students must carry. And it is a mark of faith that suffering may make us kinder, more loving people.

—Hannah Cushing

High School Language Arts Teacher for students with
emotional and behavioral disorders
Minnetonka, Minnesota

Kindness

Before you know what kindness really is
you must lose things,
feel the future dissolve in a moment
like salt in a weakened broth.
What you held in your hand,
what you counted and carefully saved,
all this must go so you know
how desolate the landscape can be
between the regions of kindness.
How you ride and ride
thinking the bus will never stop,
the passengers eating maize and chicken
will stare out the window forever.

Before you learn the tender gravity of kindness,
you must travel where the Indian in a white poncho
lies dead by the side of the road.
You must see how this could be you,
how he too was someone
who journeyed through the night with plans
and the simple breath that kept him alive.

Before you know kindness as the deepest thing inside,
you must know sorrow as the other deepest thing.
You must wake up with sorrow.
You must speak to it till your voice
catches the thread of all sorrows
and you see the size of the cloth.

Then it is only kindness that makes sense anymore,
only kindness that ties your shoes
and sends you out into the day to mail letters and purchase bread,
only kindness that raises its head
from the crowd of the world to say
It is I you have been looking for,
and then goes with you everywhere
like a shadow or a friend.

—*Naomi Shihab Nye*

Following the Boston Marathon bombing, the communities where I live and teach were on "lockdown" as police searched for the suspects. During those surreal days, I grappled with what to say to my own children, ages nine and eleven. I worried about how my high school students would respond.

As a mother and teacher, I find it tricky to balance kids' right to know difficult truths with my own yearning to protect them. Margaret Atwood's poem acknowledges the predicament of navigating a child's dawning awareness that the world is complicated, often sad, sometimes murky—and that adults don't have the answers.

It offers a pretty clear strategy: honor *and* comfort their pain. Don't turn away from a kid's darkness. Do point them back to those elemental things that can both anchor and release them: their own creative authority, the power of words and art, and the love of those who will bear witness to it all.

When school reconvened, my students expressed a range of reactions: scared, bewildered, numb, blustery, and full of bravado. Behind it all, though, I think they just wanted to know they were safe.

"You Begin" reminds us, in its beautiful and ruthless way, of our duty to try to translate a world that often doesn't make sense. It reminds us to keep our kids company no matter what. It reminds us of our limits; in the end, it says, all we can really do is hold their hand in our hand. And in the end, it turns out, that is a lot.

—*Karen Harris*

High School English Teacher
Brookline, Massachusetts

You Begin

You begin this way:
this is your hand,
this is your eye,
that is a fish, blue and flat
on the paper, almost
the shape of an eye.
This is your mouth, this is an O
or a moon, whichever
you like. This is yellow.

Outside the window
is the rain, green
because it is summer, and beyond that
the trees and then the world,
which is round and has only
the colors of these nine crayons.

This is the world, which is fuller
and more difficult to learn than I have said.
You are right to smudge it that way
with the red and then
the orange: the world burns.

Once you have learned these words
you will learn that there are more
words than you can ever learn.
The word *hand* floats above your hand
like a small cloud over a lake.
The word *hand* anchors
your hand to this table,
your hand is a warm stone
I hold between two words.

This is your hand, these are my hands, this is the world,
which is round but not flat and has more colors
than we can see.

It begins, it has an end,
this is what you will
come back to, this is your hand.

—*Margaret Atwood*

In the past decade, the pressures on teachers and students have intensified. We have less permission to take the time to "read" our students, pursue interesting detours in the curriculum, or develop genuine connections, and so the tension mounts. I have witnessed a growing anger, particularly toward students who act out in class and who hold classrooms hostage with both subtle and flagrant resistance.

I come back to this poem to be a better teacher and revisit my core belief that, as teachers, we need to have empathy for our rule-breakers who can kidnap our attention by strutting their stuff, putting on an attitude, or riling the more vulnerable. The solutions dwell not in zero-tolerance policies, but in class work that encourages sharing and understanding how others feel.

A setting where I have experienced success in cultivating a capacity for empathy is in writing workshops where we comment on what works—what we notice and like about a classmate's piece. We practice active listening and constructive responses. Thus, even when blood is dripping and murder and mayhem reign in someone's writing, I strain, but yes, I note interesting details and powerful verbs that build tension. The other students follow suit. Our reader follows the ritual and responds with an authentic thank-you because he or she feels genuinely heard and acknowledged. We are all practicing empathy.

So, back I go to the poem, taking up the invitation to call myself by other names. To think of myself as a rule breaker so that I can perhaps see their true needs and open "the door of compassion."

—*Ruth Charney*

Retired Teacher and Co-founder
Northeast Foundation for Children and Responsive Classroom
Greenfield, Massachusetts

Please Call Me by My True Names

Don't say that I will depart tomorrow—
even today I am still arriving.

Look deeply: every second I am arriving
to be a bud on a Spring branch,
to be a tiny bird, with still-fragile wings,
learning to sing in my new nest,
to be a caterpillar in the heart of a flower,
to be a jewel hiding itself in a stone.

I still arrive, in order to laugh and to cry,
to fear and to hope.
The rhythm of my heart is the birth and death
of all that is alive.

I am the mayfly metamorphosing
on the surface of the river.
And I am the bird
that swoops down to swallow the mayfly.

I am the frog swimming happily
in the clear water of a pond.
And I am the grass-snake
that silently feeds itself on the frog.

I am the child in Uganda, all skin and bones,
my legs as thin as bamboo sticks.
And I am the arms merchant,
selling deadly weapons to Uganda.

I am the twelve-year-old girl,
refugee on a small boat,
who throws herself into the ocean
after being raped by a sea pirate.
And I am the pirate,
my heart not yet capable
of seeing and loving.

I am a member of the politburo,
with plenty of power in my hands.
And I am the man who has to pay
his "debt of blood" to my people
dying slowly in a forced-labor camp.

My joy is like Spring, so warm
it makes flowers bloom in all over the Earth.
My pain is like a river of tears,
so vast it fills the four oceans.

Please call me by my true names,
so I can hear all my cries and laughter at once,
so I can see that my joy and pain are one.

Please call me by my true names,
so I can wake up
and the door of my heart
could be left open,
the door of compassion.

—Thich Nhat Hanh

He was a slip of a boy, small for his age. A ninth grader often mistaken for a fifth or sixth. He had that bright and wild sensibility about him. The wonder in the eyes and energy in the step that we often see in kids labeled "ADHD." Sometimes after school a group of boys and I would go hike in the woods behind the campus. On those days he was so full of questions. Questions about the forest or the sky or the birds, or why that tree had died or this one had not. Often the questions came so fast that I couldn't answer one before the next was upon us.

Sometimes I would glance through the small windows in the classroom door, watching him squirm, trying to sit still for forty-three minutes and listen to a history lecture or a math lesson. I could see him straining to focus, trying to keep the questions inside, for he knew they were not welcome in that room. The other teachers would shake their head at conference time. "He is failing all his classes, except PE of course," always followed by nervous laughter.

I came to realize that he did not need or even want answers; his gold was in the questions themselves. As if an answer would steal away that gold, take the magic from the question. I wondered then about the gold, about the world, and about God. Wondered if we, his teachers, could ever let his gold be the glory it was, just let it be kept by God.

—*Michael Poutiatine*
College Professor of Leadership
Spokane, Washington

Deciding

One mine the Indians worked had
gold so good they left it there
for God to keep.

At night sometimes you think
your way that far, that deep,
or almost.

You hold all things or not, depending
not on greed but whether they suit what
life begins to mean.

Like those workers you study what moves,
what stays. You bow, and then, like them,
you know—

What's God, what's world, what's gold.

—William Stafford

When, as a poet-in-residence, I visit classes (primary grades through high school), I include Li-Young Lee's "Eating Together" as a model poem because it evokes emotions that matter—in this memory piece, the missing and missed father. As the students share their losses of objects, pets, and family members, their memories stir me to think of my German grandfather who died one winter during my childhood. On visits to us, he'd smoke a pipe; he liked to go to South Beach. This was long ago—during World War II; back then, loss was kept inside.

After we discover elements of poetry in a rereading of the poem, I ask them to close their eyes and think of a house, its rooms, and find something—an object, like the trout in the poem, that might remind them of someone. I suggest going outside, anywhere, to seek what may be found. Pencils begin to move. They share, and the magic and mystery of poetry begin. By week's end, they're running after me in the halls: "I have another 'What I Saw' poem."

On the last day, many say they will not forget the poem's closing, "Then he lay down / to sleep like a snow-covered road . . ." And I think of a student with special needs who didn't participate, look up, or make eye contact, and how as I sat with him and asked if he remembered a place, an occasion, he mumbled answers to my questions:

"Island Beach State Park.
My mom and dad, brother and sister.
We went to spread my grandpa's ashes.
I carried the urn."

—*Wanda S. Praisner*

Poet-in-Residence
Bedminster, New Jersey

Eating Together

In the steamer is the trout
seasoned with slivers of ginger,
two sprigs of green onion, and sesame oil.
We shall eat it with rice for lunch,
brothers, sister, my mother who will
taste the sweetest meat of the head,
holding it between her fingers
deftly, the way my father did
weeks ago. Then he lay down
to sleep like a snow-covered road
winding through pines older than him,
without any travelers, and lonely for no one.

—*Li-Young Lee*

In 1993 I began teaching in a remote mountain community in Yaak Valley, Montana, where for four years I taught just eight to twelve students. So when I first moved "down to town" to teach English in a high school of two hundred kids, I was terrified.

My first day ended in exhaustion. As the bell rang, one young lad, Jeff, called out to me, "See you, Mr. Henderson; enjoyed class." I was amazed and thrilled—Was he serious? The next day—same thing. He did it every day. I grew to count on him more than he'll ever know. I also came to know that Jeff had serious learning disabilities and struggled every day to do what other kids did with ease or at least apathy. But he was the one who taught me the power of words of encouragement as I struggled to break through these new frontiers.

Two years later, I was the principal of this high school and it was commencement. After it was over, Jeff walked up to me holding his diploma and disposable mortarboard. He looked up at me and asked, "Mr. Henderson, do you want these now, or should we turn them in later?"

I started crying right there on the spot and hugged him, saying, "Jeff, those are yours forever, and no one will ever take them from you." Jeff has always been for me a "quiet miracle"—a "sacred gift woven around the heart of wonder." From where does such love come?

—*David Henderson*
College Professor of Educational Leadership
Bozeman, Montana

Blessing: For Presence

Awaken to the mystery of being here
and enter the quiet immensity of your own presence.

Have joy and peace in the temple of your senses.

Receive encouragement when new frontiers beckon.

Respond to the call of your gift and the courage to
    follow its path.

Let the flame of anger free you of all falsity.

May warmth of heart keep your presence aflame.

May anxiety never linger about you.

May your outer dignity mirror an inner dignity of
    soul.

Take time to celebrate the quiet miracles that seek
    no attention.

Be consoled in the secret symmetry of your soul.

May you experience each day as a sacred gift woven
    around the heart of wonder.

—*John O'Donohue*

This poem takes me back to my second year of teaching when I let my heart lead me "off the plank."

His name was Cory. The toughest kid in the school. The one all the teachers complained about. He was difficult to manage; he often skipped school; and when he did show up, he appeared to take pleasure in disrupting class.

Lying awake one night trying to solve the "Cory problem," I wondered what it must be like to be Cory. I tried to imagine what it must be like to show up every day in a place where no one was happy to see you, to feel the tension that seeped into people's bodies when you were around, to see the unspoken rejection in their faces. I could feel his awful loneliness, and my heart hurt.

When Cory next attended class, I genuinely smiled, walked over and put an arm around him, and said, "I am so happy to see you, Cory. I missed you." How that reception transformed him was beyond what I could have predicted. How it transformed me was even more unexpected. I saw firsthand that love is the ground for learning, and every child is a "galaxy with skin." Cory led me back to my heart.

To be a teacher is to be "standing above a mysterious fire." The poem reminds me to focus on what matters in a system full of "feeble preoccupations." It reminds me that all my students, like Cory, come alive when they are called by their true name.

—*Lianne Raymond*
High School Psychology Teacher
Courtenay, British Columbia, Canada

Your Other Name

If your life doesn't often make you feel
like a cauldron of swirling light—

If you are not often enough a woman standing
above a mysterious fire,
lifting her head to the sky—

You are doing too much, and listening too little.

Read poems. Walk in the woods. Make slow art.
Tie a rope around your heart, be led by it off the plank,
happy prisoner.

You are no animal. You are galaxy with skin.
Home to blue and yellow lightshots,
making speed-of-light curves and racecar turns,
bouncing in ricochet—

Don't slow down the light and turn it into matter
with feeble preoccupations.

Don't forget your true name:
Presiding one. Home for the gleaming.
Strong cauldron for the feast of light.

Strong cauldron for the feast of light:
I am speaking to you.
I beg you not to forget.

—*Tara Sophia Mohr*

From the first moment I heard this poem, the words spoke to my tired teacher-soul. They spoke to me as I woke each morning long before the sun, kissed my children good-bye, and started my long drive to school.

Like every teacher, every day, I joined my students in their world. A world that sent me sleepy children, brilliant children, hungry children, energetic children, angry children, sad children, and joyful children. Children who came to school yearning to learn and seeking stability and structure in their young lives. Twenty-five different needs to be met and each one deserving the best of me.

I knew how important it was for me to greet each child each day with a smile. This poem said it all to me. Each day is a new day. Forget what happened yesterday. Each and every day, every child and every teacher deserves a chance to see "life with energy and hope."

I loved the poem so much that I shared it with my class of four-year-old students each day in our morning meeting. The kids loved it, and to my delight, they began to recite it with me. We wanted to thank the author, so we made a video, laughing and reciting his poem. I retired last year, and I still look at that video, remembering those children, many of whom now have children of their own—and I still hope that each day brings them "a chance to try again."

—Jane Zalkin

Retired Elementary School Teacher
Charleston, South Carolina

Good Morning!

I love the way a new day feels.
Those few moments when
Yesterday's memories
Are slept into a docile file for later.
When rest gives birth to new eyes
That see a life with energy and hope
And a chance to try again.

—*Jim R. Rogers*

As a teacher, I often think my work is "to reteach a thing its loveliness." My students show up in my classroom filled with self-doubt, with harsh self-evaluations, with stories about unworthiness and not-enoughness for which they often compensate with cockiness and bravado. They have been told, in an enormous number of ways, that they aren't good enough, aren't smart enough—or else they absorb the message that winning the game of school is all that matters—and underneath they've become anxious and cynical.

As teachers, we sometimes have glimpses of the greatness that lies beneath this accreted shell, the budding flower that lies below the hard, spiny spikiness. In some teaching moments—when we're present and quiet and settled in ourselves—we are given the gift of seeing our students, of observing something they don't see in themselves. It is our work to bear witness to that—to help them catch glimpses of themselves and their own great promise.

I know from my own experience that when a teacher really listened to my story, it was a muted beginning of compassion for myself and my own strained and misfitting early life. I began to discover my own sense of sureness beneath the unsureness, of the power of showing up as myself, however flawed, unglamorous, and hollow-core doored that might be. This poem reminds me that we all need someone to bear witness to us; to listen with quiet spiritual presence; or to cheer us on, to help us remember, snout to tail down our thick length, our emergent and eternal loveliness.

—*Kirsten Olson*

Founding Member
Institute for Democratic Education in America
Brookline, Massachusetts

Saint Francis and the Sow

The bud
stands for all things,
even for those things that don't flower,
for everything flowers, from within, of self-blessing;
though sometimes it is necessary
to reteach a thing its loveliness,
to put a hand on its brow
of the flower
and retell it in words and in touch
it is lovely
until it flowers again from within, of self-blessing;
as Saint Francis
put his hand on the creased forehead
of the sow, and told her in words and in touch
blessings of earth on the sow, and the sow
began remembering all down her thick length,
from the earthen snout all the way
through the fodder and slops to the spiritual curl of the tail,
from the hard spininess spiked out from the spine
down through the great broken heart
to the blue milken dreaminess spurting and shuddering
from the fourteen teats into the fourteen mouths sucking and blowing
    beneath them:
the long, perfect loveliness of sow.

—*Galway Kinnell*

The Work Is Hard

*T*he sheer intensity of a teacher's workload takes its toll. The daily grind of preparing lessons, managing a busy classroom, giving feedback on student work, and juggling multiple commitments to the school community leaves teachers feeling weary and depleted. In addition, teachers face unrelenting external pressure to prepare students to take standardized tests, implement the required yet always changing curriculum, and institute the latest learning fad.

These outside forces buffet teachers, but because so many teachers are called to the profession by a genuine passion to make a difference and help others learn, they also face the pressure of meeting their own expectations. Teachers spend many hours planning and preparing, intending to be excellent for their students, and to live up to their own standard of craftsmanship and purpose. They care fervidly about doing right by their students—particularly their most vulnerable.

The teachers in this section contend with what it means to be excellent in work that is uncertain and unpredictable. They consider what it means to make peace with imperfection, errors, mistakes, and the uneven realities of classroom life. They give voice to their fear and the sense of vulnerability that come from doing work that is highly public, and scrutinized, and that continually demands emotional exposure.

My teaching life has often been shaped by the anguish of self-doubt. As a new teacher, I would wonder, *What am I doing? Why did I use the strategy that fell flat with this class? Why did I use sarcasm with that child? Shouldn't a teacher know what to do each minute, in every circumstance?* The learning curve was long and steep, and at times I felt like a fraud.

Over the years, I have grown toward becoming a master teacher, and I have found tremendous satisfaction in my students' growth and success. And the teaching part has gotten easier; I know I am good at what I do. Yet I am still painfully aware of the mistakes I make each day. Doubt can still hover over me.

When I remember that I need to stop obsessing, that I need to pause and move on, I reach for Antonio Machado's poem, which I know as "Caminante." There, like a walk on a beach, he gently offers me hope, a reminder of the redemption that may come with each footstep of life. Machado whispers to me, "Mike, live for the present moment, not the past. Release the stress and all that self-doubt. Look back at your *huellas*, those footprints behind you; watch as they disappear like foam trails in the sea."

In the zenith of my career, I am fortunately becoming the *caminante*, the wayfarer, and gradually trusting the path I am on, as I walk it.

—*Michael L. Crauderueff*
High School Spanish Teacher
Wynnewood, Pennsylvania

VI

Caminante, son tus huellas
el camino, y nada más;
caminante, no hay camino,
se hace camino al andar.
Al andar se hace camino,
y al volver la vista atrás
se ve la senda que nunca
se ha de volver a pisar.
Caminante, no hay camino,
sino estelas en la mar.

Wayfarer, the only way
is your footsteps, there is no other.
Wayfarer, there is no way,
you make the way as you go.
As you go, you make the way
and stopping to look behind,
you see the path that your feet
will never travel again.
Wayfarer, there is no way—
Only foam trails in the sea.

—Antonio Machado

I often feel guilty. I feel guilty about not writing more feedback on student work, not making more phone calls to parents, not paying more attention to the subtle signals my students send me about what they need.

I used to embrace that guilt—almost harvest it—because I thought it pushed me to become a more perfect teacher. But at some point, I realized that my guilt erodes my love and passion for teaching. Worn out and chagrined by what I haven't done, I become cranky and distant in the classroom.

This poem insists that I let it go. It connects me to things beyond my windowless classroom: the sun and clear pebbles of rain; prairies and deep trees; the clean, blue air. It helps me remember that there is a whole world out there.

The thing I love best about the poem is the last five lines. Teaching can be lonely, isolating. This poem reminds me that no matter how lonely I may be, what happens inside my classroom can conjure up possibilities and make it a place where the world offers itself to our imagination. I invite students to write about their lives outside of school, and together we read about the worlds beyond our classroom. I realize that my students are the wild geese, calling to me in a way that can be "harsh," but also "exciting." I want them, many of whom also are lonely, to know that they too have a "place in the family of things."

—*Kathleen Melville*

High School English and Spanish Teacher
Philadelphia, Pennsylvania

Wild Geese

You do not have to be good.
You do not have to walk on your knees
for a hundred miles through the desert, repenting.
You only have to let the soft animal of your body
   love what it loves.
Tell me about despair, yours, and I will tell you mine.
Meanwhile the world goes on.
Meanwhile the sun and the clear pebbles of the rain
are moving across the landscapes,
over the prairies and the deep trees,
the mountains and the rivers.
Meanwhile the wild geese, high in the clean blue air,
are heading home again.
Whoever you are, no matter how lonely,
the world offers itself to your imagination,
calls to you like the wild geese, harsh and exciting—
over and over announcing your place
in the family of things.

—Mary Oliver

It's just after spring break when I scrawl this poem on the whiteboard. We are three-quarters through the school year, but for many students it feels like it's already over. For the dejected and the defeated, the ones whose grades are irredeemable, there's little reason to try. And even for me, their teacher with the irrepressible optimism, it seems a bit more difficult to persist, to insist that all of my students continue to give their all. So up it goes, a reminder to us all that we need—no matter what—to "press on."

My classroom walls are covered with evidence of persistence from literary figures like Stephen King and J. K. Rowling, entrepreneurs like Walt Disney, scientists like Albert Einstein, political figures like Abraham Lincoln, and sports heroes like Michael Jordan, all of whom overcame obstacles through diligence and determination.

But there's something about the fourth quarter of the school year that needs that solid, obstinate, in-your-face declaration that talent, genius, and education alone do not seal the deal. It's dogged persistence in the face of adversity—the refusal to give up—that wins the day.

I may teach literary analysis and close reading strategies, but day in and day out I teach students these survival skills, this resilience, this refusal to give up the dream. I teach grit.

And when I'm tempted—to accept less on an assignment or to look the other way, or, heaven forbid, to give up on a student—these words echo in my head: "Nothing in the world can take the place of persistence."

—*April Niemela*
Middle and High School English Language Arts Teacher
Lewiston, Idaho

Persistence

Nothing in the world can take the place of persistence.

Talent will not; nothing is more common than unsuccessful men with talent.

Genius will not; unrewarded genius is almost a proverb.

Education will not; the world is full of educated derelicts.

Persistence and determination alone are omnipotent.

The slogan "press on" has solved and always will solve the problems of the human race.

—*Calvin Coolidge*

Given to me my freshman year of college, this poem meant nothing until I moved to New York City to teach. After years of teaching, I rediscovered the poem one weeknight while preparing for a lesson and found the story strikingly familiar.

Spending my entire professional life as a teacher in a classroom of all minority students has changed me, but I struggle to articulate how these changes affect even the most pedestrian elements of my life, such as riding the subway. When I am in the classroom, my students are my students; regardless of race, language, religion, or ethnicity, we form a community. It is a deep bond.

But outside the classroom, my racism rises like an old habit. How can I love the students I teach but fall prey to unsubstantiated fear when a black kid wearing all red sits across from me on the subway? That makes no sense. I realize this. It still happens. When it does, I feel befuddled, depressed, exhausted by my hypocrisy.

I think about this. A lot. This poem narrates one of my many subway rides. I see a young man, I see me. I see the power we both have and how society defines that power and privilege. But I also see what the poet does not see: I see the young man as a student of mine, and then—and only then—I see love. Deep in these thoughts, I'll catch his eye and smile. And, most of the time, he smiles back.

—*Lori Ungemah*
Founding Faculty Member
Guttman Community College
New York, New York

On the Subway

The boy and I face each other.
His feet are huge, in black sneakers
laced with white in a complex pattern like a
set of intentional scars. We are stuck on
opposite sides of the car, a couple of
molecules stuck in a rod of light
rapidly moving through darkness. He has the
casual cold look of a mugger,
alert under hooded lids. He is wearing
red, like the inside of the body
exposed. I am wearing dark fur, the
whole skin of an animal taken and
used. I look at his raw face,
he looks at my fur coat, and I don't
know if I am in his power—
he could take my coat so easily, my
briefcase, my life—
or if he is in my power, the way I am
living off his life, eating the steak
he does not eat, as if I am taking
the food from his mouth. And he is black
and I am white, and without meaning or
trying to I must profit from his darkness,
the way he absorbs the murderous beams of the
nation's heart, as black cotton
absorbs the heat of the sun and holds it. There is
no way to know how easy this

white skin makes my life, this
life he could take so easily and
break across his knee like a stick the way his
own back is being broken, the
rod of his soul that at birth was dark and
fluid and rich as the heart of a seeding
ready to thrust up into any available light.

—*Sharon Olds*

Someone gave my brother, Danny, this poem and a pair of work gloves at dawn before he began work on a farm one day, sunup to sundown. I can't let it go. I tape it to office doors and share it with my students—future teachers.

I teach a class for student teachers, and for weeks we talk about how and when people learn; and then one day, we imagine ourselves as teachers in a school. We have promised to extend students' understanding and appreciation of certain difficult concepts we have read about in contemporary nonfiction, problems related to the legacy of Jim Crow, American food production, radiation, cancer, and Hurricane Katrina. As if we were in a five-ring circus, the future teachers simultaneously teach forty-two-minute lessons in five different "classrooms" of their peers. Before the first "bell" rings, I read "Work Gloves" to calm their nerves and to express my gratitude for our profession.

In my first year of teaching, when June came, the sadness upended me. So much could have been better. My department head consoled me, "Each September you start fresh." Now, years later, the beauty I see in teaching lies in the cycles of dreaming, hoping, experimenting, revising, and taking satisfaction in the process. At night I take off my work gloves, and slowly review what I want to remember from the day. Life goes fast, and this poem reminds me to be present and thankful for the opportunity to try my best, and to let each day be something good.

—*Tom Meyer*
College Professor of Education
New Paltz, New York

Work Gloves

This is the beginning of a new day.
What you do today is important because
You are exchanging a day of your life for it . . .
When tomorrow comes, this day will be gone forever;
In its place is something you've left behind.
Let it be something good.

—Anonymous

The act of teaching, when it works, is magnificent. I share what I know with my students like it is a well-crafted gift, and my students accept it like a dress that fits perfectly and flatters, or a beaded head wrap, twinkling with lights. When it works, I feel like "an emperor for a minute."

And yet, on those inevitable days when teaching doesn't work—when the great ideas I had over the weekend go over like a lead balloon—I awake at 3:00 a.m. and microanalyze every move and misstep. Blame sits on me like a fat, wet dog. *You rushed*, it slobbers in my ear. *You judged, you railroaded, you ramrodded. You didn't notice their faces, their strain, their flagging attention, or their flickers of light. You are the worst teacher ever.*

I teach special education in a treatment center. My students are "behavior" kids. They are trying to learn skills to cope with their emotional chaos along with academics. Throughout their short lives, everything has conspired to dull their light—poverty, homelessness, crappy-ass parents, drugs, learning disabilities.

The poem reminds me that we all ache, we all struggle, and we all blaze. It reminds me to notice each struggle, each effort, each glow. Each time I read this poem, I'm determined "next time" to improve my game, to slow down, and to take a breath and a long look before I open my mouth. And then "I'd know more"; I'd know that I teach to a light show.

—Leanne Grabel Sander
Special Education and Language Arts Teacher
Portland, Oregon

Next Time

Next time what I'd do is look at
the earth before saying anything. I'd stop
just before going into a house
and be an emperor for a minute
and listen better to the wind
     or to the air being still.

When anyone talked to me, whether
blame or praise or just passing time,
I'd watch the face, how the mouth
has to work, and see any strain, any
sign of what lifted the voice.

And for all, I'd know more—the earth
bracing itself and soaring, the air
finding every leaf and feather over
forest and water, and for every person
the body glowing inside the clothes
     like a light.

                  —*William Stafford*

I fell hard for Emily Dickinson in college. Her teasing ambiguity drove many of my peers crazy, but I relished trying to crack the code, looking for the secret meaning. Reading her poetry was like playing a game with no rules.

As a first-year teacher, I often feel like I'm lost in a Dickinson poem. I know so little, and there is so much that is hard to decipher. The first grinding months were overwhelming. I set aside the playfulness that had sustained me, thinking it was time to be serious. I became authoritarian and tried to create a perfect class with straight lines and silent students. I started to become "accustomed to the Dark."

It wasn't until teaching a poetry unit that I began to see my way back to the light. I couldn't help but be myself as we discussed poetry together. I wanted them to experience the delight of poetry, to taste the poems on their tongue. Suddenly, I could appreciate the place for Dickinson-like playfulness and ambiguity in my teaching. With a new focus on experimenting and exploring together, our crooked lines through the hall didn't matter as much. It was all about where we were going together.

It is enormously freeing to know that teaching is not about creating perfect little lives; it's the imperfections and deviations that are captivating and valuable, the instances of life stepping "almost straight." My fourth graders understand how to embrace that. It's a skill that is often lost, but that can be relearned. I try to remember that.

—Rachel Fentin
Elementary School Teacher
Detroit, Michigan

We grow accustomed to the Dark–
When Light is put away–
As when the Neighbor holds the Lamp
To witness her Good bye–

A Moment–We uncertain step
For newness of the night–
Then–fit our Vision to the Dark–
And meet the Road–erect–

And so of larger–Darknesses–
Those Evenings of the Brain–
When not a Moon disclose a sign–
Or Star–come out–within–

The Bravest–grope a little–
And sometimes hit a Tree
Directly in the Forehead–
But as they learn to see–

Either the Darkness alters–
Or something in the sight
Adjusts itself to Midnight–
And Life steps almost straight.

—Emily Dickinson

Walt Whitman hears the learned astronomer with his abundance of charts, columns, and calculations, and soon feels drained and sickened. I, too, can feel weary and dispirited in my work as a college professor. This lethargy takes hold when I survey college texts, heavy of page and with an overkill of learning objectives, or when I trudge through box loads of dossiers dutifully and painstakingly assembled for tenure or promotion. The volume of detail, its sheer glut, overwhelms, until I, too, yearn to wander off and breathe "the mystical moist night-air."

Who among us has not wilted under a barrage of PowerPointed academic monologues, or felt coldly hollow when facing bureaucratic rubrics and assessment standards? Who has not winced at long-winded scholarship and research that offer so little help? At such moments, we silently scream at the gap between the abstractions of our discourse and life itself, including the world within which our students live and move. Each of us in our own way and time, if sensitivity be ours, shares Whitman's nausea at the gulfs between symbols and the real deal.

And like Whitman, from time to time, we glide past the rigorous propriety of sanctioned learnedness and gaze "in perfect silence at the stars." Standing beside Whitman, we rise in awe at the beautiful elusiveness of the subject matter that beguiled us years ago, and once again open our hearts to the true uniqueness and ultimate immeasurability of each of our students. Heart, head, and hand united, we *reach*.

And then, we *teach*.

—Ronald Gordon

College Professor of Communication
Hilo, Hawai'i

When I Heard the Learn'd Astronomer

When I heard the learn'd astronomer,
When the proofs, the figures, were ranged in columns before me,
When I was shown the charts and diagrams, to add, divide, and
  measure them,
When I sitting heard the astronomer where he lectured with much
  applause in the lecture-room,
How soon unaccountable I became tired and sick,
Till rising and gliding out I wander'd off by myself,
In the mystical moist night-air, and from time to time,
Look'd up in perfect silence at the stars.

—Walt Whitman

Prior to teaching, I was a modern dancer. Waiting in the wings for my cue to enter the stage, I would agonize about forgetting the steps I rehearsed, losing my balance, or tripping. Teaching is now my performance, and the classroom is my stage. In teaching, I experience a similar blend of terror and exhilaration before class. I worry that I'm not prepared enough, that I won't remember the nuances of what I want students to learn, that the students won't be engaged, that I'll flop.

Wislawa Szymborska's poem shifts my perspective. No matter how prepared, I must be attentive to the present moment and ready for the unpredictable. Each time I read the poem, I feel less alone in my fear; I lighten up a bit.

Lightening up opens up opportunities for spontaneity and improvisation. When I was a dancer, if I forgot what came next, I'd keep moving, improvising until I found my way back to the choreography as planned. Similarly, in teaching, if what I've prepared doesn't seem to work, I adjust in the moment, changing the focus or creating a different activity.

By lightening up, I am able to see myself and others with "soft eyes." Without compassion for myself, it would be hard for me to have compassion for my students. Creating a caring environment supports their learning. It is the most important thing I can do. For, as Szymborska reminds me, whatever I do in the classroom lives forever in the lives of my students.

—*Veta Goler*

College Professor of Dance
Atlanta, Georgia

Life While-You-Wait

Life While-You-Wait.
Performance without rehearsal.
Body without alterations.
Head without premeditation.

I know nothing of the role I play.
I only know it's mine, I can't exchange it.

I have to guess on the spot
just what this play's all about.

Ill-prepared for the privilege of living,
I can barely keep up with the pace that the action demands.
I improvise, although I loathe improvisation.
I trip at every step over my own ignorance.
I can't conceal my hayseed manners.
My instincts are for hammy histrionics.
Stage fright makes excuses for me, which humiliate me more.
Extenuating circumstances strike me as cruel.

Words and impulses you can't take back,
stars you'll never get counted,
your character like a raincoat you button on the run—
the pitiful results of all this unexpectedness.

If I could just rehearse one Wednesday in advance,
or repeat a single Thursday that has passed!
But here comes Friday with a script I haven't seen.
Is it fair, I ask
(my voice a little hoarse,
since I couldn't even clear my throat offstage).

You'd be wrong to think that it's just a slapdash quiz
taken in makeshift accommodations. Oh no.
I'm standing on the set and I see how strong it is.
The props are surprisingly precise.
The machine rotating the stage has been around even longer.
The farthest galaxies have been turned on.
Oh no, there's no question, this must be the premiere.
And whatever I do
will become forever what I've done.

—*Wislawa Szymborska*

Tenacity

*A*t a time when there is increasing ethnic, cultural, language, and religious diversity combined with pervasive socioeconomic inequities, teachers cling to their belief in the power of education to redress long-standing struggles in our society. Teachers believe that because our schools are open and accessible to all, they are places where we can teach children to become citizens who can contribute to solving the fundamental challenges of our time.

Through the poems and commentaries in this section, teachers reveal how seriously they take the task of helping students learn to be active and engaged citizens. Teachers value the role of the school in building a strong and just democracy and assert, as did Eleanor Roosevelt, that the quest to achieve human dignity must begin in our most ordinary and familiar places. In a speech to the United Nations, Roosevelt asked, "Where, after all, do universal human rights begin? In small places, close to home—so close and so small that they cannot be seen on any maps of the world. Yet they are the world of the individual person; the neighborhood he lives in; the school or college he attends; the factory, farm, or office where he works."[1] Teachers live this philosophy each day.

---

1. E. Roosevelt, "In Your Hands" (speech, United Nations, New York, March 27, 1958), http://www.milestone documents.com/documents/view/eleanor-roosevelts-remarks-at-the-united-nations-concerning-human -rights/text.

I grew up on the Lower East Side in New York City. My pre-gentrification neighborhood didn't accommodate the twee bakeries and cafes now propped all along the blocks. Rather, the streets were strewn with dime bags and multicolored tops for crack, cocaine, and weed, and the homeless sought the protection of the walls throughout the cold winters.

At night, I often slept to the din made by thugs with their nocturnal activities. A few times a month, gunfire would shake our eardrums, and our consciousness. Rats routinely scurried in between the walls, in crevices left open, through the metal pipes for the heater.

By day, I found refuge eating Frosted Flakes in a huge bowl of milk, watching Power Rangers, and excelling at school. I was lucky to have a mother who knew that an education could provide me with endless possibilities and inspired and pushed me to do well. School felt like a second home, and I took comfort in its routines.

Now, as a teacher, I'm reminded that my students understand struggle as I did then. Our shared experience motivates my teaching, and I try to help them dream so that they can "learn to breathe fresh air." But I wonder, how can people from the outside looking in tell children in desperate poverty that their first priority must be their education? How many of us can find the right balance between academic achievement and human empathy, not just in the slums of New York City, but also in Chicago, Kabul, Mumbai, Port-au-Prince, and Sarajevo?

—Jose Vilson
Middle School Math Teacher, Speaker, and Activist
New York, New York

The Rose That Grew from Concrete

Did u hear about the rose that grew from a crack
in the concrete
Proving nature's laws wrong it learned 2 walk
without having feet
Funny it seems but by keeping its dreams
it learned 2 breathe fresh air
Long live the rose that grew from concrete
when no one else even cared!

—Tupac Shakur

The late 1980s, Team English, early in September, in a suburb north of Detroit. Eighty squirming, sweating ninth graders in a large classroom. My department chair, Henry Maloney; the drama teacher, Linda Petranek; and I launched a litera-ture-based study on the purposes of education. We acted out Philip Levine's poem. Dr. Maloney played Monsieur Degas with a flourish, pacing and pausing. Linda and I voiced the parts of students, acting out their puzzlement, tossing our heads and leaning out into the aisles. Drama? Substance? In school? We got their attention.

When young people encounter an artist—a doer, a maker, a writer—in a class-room, there is cognitive dissonance. There is "bucking and quaking" on every-body's part as the artist-teacher "begins to separate the dark from the dark." I've heard Levine speak about the French teacher who inspired the poem. He talked about the gap between the man's intellectual life and the lives of the Detroit chil-dren—including a young Levine—he was trying to engage. Levine admired the French teacher's persistent kindness.

The poem was an elegy for an era and a city when it was published in 1991 in *What Work Is*. Now, as I drive past burned-out row houses and dilapidated man-sions on my way to a Detroit high school, not far from Durfee, the elegiac aspect takes on new life. So does the urgency. This struggling city and its youth need passionate, deeply knowledgeable teachers who open new worlds. More than ever. Foreign as that might seem.

—*Laura Roop*
Director of Outreach
University of Michigan School of Education
Ann Arbor, Michigan

M. Degas Teaches Art & Science at Durfee Intermediate School, Detroit, 1942

He made a line on the blackboard,
one bold stroke from right to left
diagonally downward and stood back
to ask, looking as always at no one
in particular, "What have I done?"
From the back of the room Freddie
shouted, "You've broken a piece
of chalk." M. Degas did not smile.
"What have I done?" he repeated.
The most intellectual students
looked down to study their desks
except for Gertrude Bimmler, who raised
her hand before she spoke. "M. Degas,
you have created the hypotenuse
of an isosceles triangle." Degas mused.
Everyone knew that Gertrude could not
be incorrect. "It is possible,"
Louis Warshowsky added precisely,
"that you have begun to represent
the roof of a barn." I remember
that it was exactly twenty minutes
past eleven, and I thought at worst
this would go on another forty
minutes. It was early April,
the snow had all but melted on
the playgrounds, the elms and maples

bordering the cracked walks shivered
in the new winds, and I believed
that before I knew it I'd be
swaggering to the candy store
for a Milky Way. M. Degas
pursed his lips, and the room
stilled until the long hand
of the clock moved to twenty one
as though in complicity with Gertrude,
who added confidently, "You've begun
to separate the dark from the dark."
I looked back for help, but now
the trees bucked and quaked, and I
knew this could go on forever.

—Philip Levine

In 1990 Boston was second only to Los Angeles in youth violence. Our city neighborhoods were rough, and the young people living there were desperate, unable to lead a kid's life or escape the violence.

I believed making art could bring relief, that the magic of the creative process could reconnect them to their innocence and awaken the kind of curiosity that inspires learning.

The work of making art is independent, entrepreneurial, and available to all. Understanding the relationship of art to life, as work is to love, is to know why we are here, living. Being an artist and making these connections have shaped my reality. I have lived in faith that the creative process will be there for me against all odds. This is the defining power I wanted to share.

My vision was to inspire teens to engage in the creative process and participate in commerce. My intent was to communicate their experiences to the larger world through the creation and marketing of their collaborative works, thereby empowering them, providing them with an income, and educating their community.

I found young people hungry for this opportunity. They came every day after school. In the summer, they sat on the steps outside my studio. At night I drove them home. Artists For Humanity began with this entrepreneurial venture and now employs hundreds of teen artists. The story of this poem and of my own journey affirms what is possible when we help young people take ownership of their talent to learn, create, share, love, and live.

—Susan Rodgerson
Founder and Director
Artists For Humanity
Boston, Massachusetts

Struggle

It's a struggle
Developing Solidarity.
It's a struggle
Being Positive
It's a struggle
Making Common Unity.
It's a struggle
LIVING.
It's a struggle
Because it's slow
But if we Struggle
At developing Solidarity,
Being Positive
Shaping Reality,
Making Common Unity,
We will all Grow
Because to struggle
Is to work for Change,
and Change is the focus of Education,
and Education is the Basis of Knowledge,
and Knowledge is the Basis for Growth
and Growth is the Basis for
Being Positive and Being Positive
is the Basis for Building Solidarity
Building Solidarity is a way to shape
Reality and Shaping Reality is Living
and Living is Loving,
So Struggle.

—*Mel King*

I was born in the Dominican Republic surrounded by palm trees and sand. When I was five, I moved to New York City to live among the skyscrapers and asphalt. Such a beginning made me strong and resourceful.

My new neighborhood was one of the poorest areas of our country. But I never felt excluded or different. It wasn't until I started teaching at a white, upper-middle-class Boston public charter school that I struggled with the dynamics of privilege. At this school, the grass seemed greener. The students appeared happier. Amid all the white, I felt "brown." Amid all the rich, I was, for the first time, obviously poor. Witnessing the enrichment and education that come to young people with resources, I understood how being poor had affected my life.

From the first bell to the last, my first day of teaching, I knew I had been sold a broken dream. I found myself teaching students who had so much more than me, yet were made insecure by my differences, my culture, and my color. Some could not see that they could "learn from me."

But I was determined to teach and wouldn't let them meddle with my passion or my teacher's heart. Although I've broken the barrier and I've earned their respect, for some I am still the brown woman that they can't and won't try to understand. Little do they know that they are as much a part of me as I am a part of them.

—Paola Tineo

High School Spanish Teacher
Boston, Massachusetts

Theme for English B

The instructor said,

> Go home and write
> a page tonight.
> And let that page come out of you—
> Then, it will be true.

I wonder if it's that simple?
I am twenty-two, colored, born in Winston-Salem.
I went to school there, then Durham, then here
to this college on the hill above Harlem.
I am the only colored student in my class.
The steps from the hill lead down into Harlem,
through a park, then I cross St. Nicholas,
Eighth Avenue, Seventh, and I come to the Y,
the Harlem Branch Y, where I take the elevator
up to my room, sit down, and write this page:

It's not easy to know what is true for you or me
at twenty-two, my age. But I guess I'm what
I feel and see and hear, Harlem, I hear you:
hear you, hear me—we two—you, me, talk on this page.
(I hear New York too.) Me—who?
Well, I like to eat, sleep, drink, and be in love.
I like to work, read, learn, and understand life.
I like a pipe for a Christmas present,
or records—Bessie, bop, or Bach.

I guess being colored doesn't make me *not* like
the same things other folks like who are other races.
So will my page be colored that I write?
Being me, it will not be white.
But it will be
a part of you, instructor.
You are white—
yet a part of me, as I am a part of you.
That's American.
Sometimes perhaps you don't want to be a part of me.
Nor do I often want to be a part of you.
But we are, that's true!
As I learn from you,
I guess you learn from me—
although you're older—and white—
and somewhat more free.

This is my page for English B.

—Langston Hughes

Some of the best teachers I know feel like a lone dog. Often those teachers, who go above and beyond, who truly try to teach, will find themselves feeling isolated. Professional jealousy, competition for jobs, personal issues, and resentment from teachers who are less successful create a sense that despite being in the orbit of students, teachers, administrators, and parents, teaching can be darned solitary and lonely.

I'm not talking about being cooped up in a classroom grading papers or creating lesson plans, or sitting in a deadly boring department meeting or endless staff development training. I'm talking about the reality that as a teacher, you are on your own. It's you and your students versus the rigidly prescribed curriculum and the standardized tests. It's you and your fellow teachers against student apathy, truancy, and misbehavior. It's you and the teachers' union versus members of the general public, who far too often fail to understand just how mentally, physically, and emotionally exhausting your job can be.

When that happens to me, I remember that great teachers are fighters. I read this poem to remind myself that I would rather teach well than be popular in the faculty lounge. I'd rather do what's right for my students and teach them how to think for themselves, even if it means they don't score as high on standardized exams. I would rather "waste time" incorporating the arts than create a sterile classroom where the focus is limited to children's heads alone, ignoring their hearts and souls.

—LouAnne Johnson
High School English Teacher
New Mexico

Lone Dog

I'm a lean dog, a keen dog, a wild dog, and lone;
I'm a rough dog, a tough dog, hunting on my own;
I'm a bad dog, a mad dog, teasing silly sheep;
I love to sit and bay the moon, to keep fat souls from sleep.

I'll never be a lap dog, licking dirty feet,
A sleek dog, a meek dog, cringing for my meat,
Not for me the fireside, the well-filled plate,
But shut door, and sharp stone, and cuff and kick, and hate.

Not for me the other dogs, running by my side,
Some have run a short while, but none of them would bide.
O mine is still the lone trail, the hard trail, the best,
Wide wind, and wild stars, and hunger of the quest!

—*Irene Rutherford McLeod*

And then you turn 11, 12, and 13 and all the "dark blue speed" really gets drained out of you.

Middle school was abysmal for me, a "measles of the spirit," a "chicken pox of the soul." I didn't feel like what I learned was meaningful or worthwhile. I got bored and gave up. I made poor choices, fell hard on the "sidewalks of life" and had to transfer schools. Back then, teachers were the enemies. I never had an adult look me in the eye and talk with me except for when I made my regular trips to the principal's office. It wasn't until later that I had teachers who took the time to know and understand me.

When I tell old friends that I'm a middle school teacher, most laugh. But I absolutely love working with kids, being surrounded by their musings on our crazy world. They inundate me with their touching and powerful writing. They keep me laughing with their sense of humor.

Thinking back to being bored to tears in middle school fuels me with a fire to plan engaging, meaningful, and fun lessons. As a result, I get to wrestle with tough questions about our world with my students. I get to share my favorite novels and see what connections my students make with the characters and their problems. But where it really gets good is seeing students grow as scholars and caring people—and reminding them how that same pure and good imagination that dreamed of being an "Arabian wizard" can still flourish—even after turning 10.

—Will Bangs

Middle School Humanities Teacher
Northampton, Massachusetts

On Turning Ten

The whole idea of it makes me feel
like I'm coming down with something,
something worse than any stomach ache
or the headaches I get from reading in bad light—
a kind of measles of the spirit,
a mumps of the psyche,
a disfiguring chicken pox of the soul.

You tell me it is too early to be looking back,
but that is because you have forgotten
the perfect simplicity of being one
and the beautify complexity introduced by two.
But I can lie on my bed and remember every digit.
At four I was an Arabian wizard.
I could make myself invisible
by drinking a glass of milk a certain way.
At seven I was a soldier, at nine a prince.

But now I am mostly at the window
watching the late afternoon light.
Back then it never fell so solemnly
against the side of my tree house,
and my bicycle never leaned against the garage
as it does today,
all the dark blue speed drained out of it.

This is the beginning of sadness, I say to myself,
as I walk through the universe in my sneakers.
It is time to say good-bye to my imaginary friends,
time to turn the first big number.

It seems only yesterday I used to believe
there was nothing under my skin but light.
If you cut me I could shine.
But now when I fall upon the sidewalks of life,
I skin my knees. I bleed.

—*Billy Collins*

I asked my eighth-grade class, "Who wants to go to college?" All of my students immediately raised their hands. I then asked, "How many of you believe you can do it?" Most of the hands fluttered down.

I was just a student teacher, but at that moment I recognized that classroom management and lesson planning weren't my only challenges. I had to motivate my students to believe that as long as they tried their hardest at a seemingly impossible task, the task could be done.

For this message to be meaningful, I had to make it personal. To make an impact, I couldn't only be Ms. Hamilton. I had to once again be the young girl who had dreams of college in the midst of a school environment that didn't support that dream. I had to let them see me as a young immigrant girl, being raised in a single-parent household in the Bronx, watching my mom work relentlessly to provide for me while simultaneously encouraging me to study, to work hard in everything, and to dream. Education was never presented to me as a choice. It was presented as an opportunity to shatter the statistics that would claim me as less than the potential that resided within me.

I believe there is nothing my students can't do. My job is to get my students to dream of a life and future beyond what they know. I know they can do it. And I am the proof.

—*Glendean Hamilton*
**Middle School English Student-Teacher
Springfield, Massachusetts**

It Couldn't Be Done

Somebody said that it couldn't be done,
    But he with a chuckle replied
That "maybe it couldn't," but he would be one
    Who wouldn't say so till he'd tried.
So he buckled right in with the trace of a grin
    On his face. If he worried he hid it.
He started to sing as he tackled the thing
    That couldn't be done, and he did it.

Somebody scoffed: "Oh, you'll never do that;
    At least no one ever has done it";
But he took off his coat and he took off his hat,
    And the first thing we knew he'd begun it.
With a lift of his chin and a bit of a grin,
    Without any doubting or quiddit,
He started to sing as he tackled the thing
    That couldn't be done, and he did it.

There are thousands to tell you it cannot be done,
    There are thousands to prophesy failure;
There are thousands to point out to you one by
        one,
    The dangers that wait to assail you.
But just buckle in with a bit of a grin,
    Just take off your coat and go to it;
Just start in to sing as you tackle the thing
    That "cannot be done," and you'll do it.

—Edgar A. Guest

When I was a single dad in the late 1970s, I would skip my law school classes at Boston University to support myself as a carpenter. I had a job at a settlement house, building a darkroom in the attic. Around 3:00 p.m. each day the kids came after school to play games downstairs. They heard noises and came up to see what was going on. I showed them what I was doing and how to use the tools. I started to look forward to 3:00, when I could see and work with the kids. I think that's where and when my career as a teacher began.

This was at the height of the desegregation struggles in Boston. I realized the very first day that these kids were every bit as bright as the "kids" I was with in law school. I thought if only we could engage their natural intelligence, develop their skills, and help them set their sights higher, they could achieve the same outcomes as the law school students.

Some well-intentioned people say we should have programs for the "non–college bound." But creating programs for the "non–college bound" means you've decided that someone's not going to college. I believe those kids are better served if they're not being segregated from those who are planning on going to college and the programs that serve them. You want to transform where kids are going, not replicate where they've come from.

—*Larry Rosenstock*
CEO and Founding Principal
High Tech High
San Diego, California

On Leadership

A leader is best
when people barely know that
he exists,
Not so good when people obey and
Acclaim him,
Worst when they despise him.
"Fail to honor people,
they fail to honor you;"
But of a good leader, who talks little,
When his work is done,
His aim fulfilled,
They will all say,
"We did this ourselves."

—*Lao-Tzu*

Raised in the Bronx, I always thought of myself as tough, streetwise. Then I started teaching in the South Bronx and saw my glaring stare, my gestures, my values, my adolescent struggles reflected on the faces in my classroom. For the first time I realized how dark the pit truly was.

At first the narrator's voice in "Invictus" was mine; it spoke of how hard life had been for me and the force I met it with. Then, with time, every struggle to get through to even one kid was a battle echoed in its lines, and each kid lost to one system or another was yet one more bludgeoning. I began to feel less the hero and more the ship on a harrowing voyage transporting fearless children under and through the "horror of the shade." Still, with head "unbowed," I continued, thinking that if I stopped, we would all fall to the "clutch of circumstance."

When that first group of freshmen stood as seniors in their caps and gowns, proudly smiling and beaming with conviction, I wept. The first few rows were filled with teachers, some openly crying, others discreetly wiping their cheeks. At the end, sobbing students hugged and thanked teachers for never giving up on them, and we thanked them for keeping us inspired and full of fire. In the tangle of arms and tears, "Invictus" again came to mind. I was in a room replete with unconquerable souls, indistinguishable from one another; each one a "master" and a "captain."

—*Caridad Caro*
Assistant Principal
Urban Assembly School
for Wildlife Conservation in the Bronx
New York, New York

Invictus

Out of the night that covers me,
    Black as the Pit from pole to pole,
I thank whatever gods may be
    For my unconquerable soul.

In the fell clutch of circumstance
    I have not winced nor cried aloud.
Under the bludgeonings of chance
    My head is bloody, but unbowed.

Beyond this place of wrath and tears
    Looms but the Horror of the shade,
And yet the menace of the years
    Finds, and shall find, me unafraid.

It matters not how strait the gate,
    How charged with punishments the scroll,
I am the master of my fate;
    I am the captain of my soul.

—William Ernest Henley

Feisty

*E*ducational programs, initiatives, and reform ventures do not spring fully formed into the world as functioning entities. They arise, as a wisp of an idea, when individuals decide to take on the status quo. Emboldened by their personal experience, committed to serving a particular community, or inspired to imagine a creative solution to long-standing inefficiencies or injustices, these individuals move to make their vision a reality. They lift their voice and push forward, often against great odds or stiff resistance from prevailing institutions. Over time they collect colleagues and resources, and that fragile impulse to make a difference becomes a forceful presence and an effective program in the lives of young people.

The poems and commentaries in this section honor what it takes to be a reformer and change agent in education. They describe how individuals resist agendas and mandates that violate their personal code and values and then forge ahead to make changes in the world and within the institutions they inhabit. These interventions take many forms, such as advancing an alternative message and vision; establishing an innovative school; implementing an inventive curriculum; pioneering an after-school program; or launching a new organization.

This section describes those who venture out into the field of action.

We Americans are so ambitious. We would go to any lengths to be successful. And so we have put success at the center of our education system. We falsely equate learning, a process, with achievement, a by-product of learning.

I came to know an alternative view when my mentor, Shakti Gattegno, shared this poem with me. She used the first two lines to highlight the reality of the learning situation—a place "where knowing and not knowing are equal." At first I found this idea too radical to even consider. Wasn't learning all about knowing? I came to understand that learning starts with the realization, *I don't know*. The rest of the learning process pauses periodically with some things known—we call this achievement—and some remaining unknown. There is no ending point, only more learning.

In my teaching, I recognize my students' mistakes, those manifestations of what they don't *yet* know, as an integral part of their learning process. I tell them that we are together in class to make mistakes and to work on them. This awareness creates a classroom culture in which the difference between teacher and student virtually disappears, and we all become seekers together, souls lying down in the grass of Rumi's metaphorical field.

Although this view of the learning process is not at all in tune with the current results-oriented job training model imposed by the government and the corporate publishing and testing complex, Rumi's poem reminds me that it is the right perspective.

—Hugh Birdsall

Teacher of English to speakers of other languages
Regional Multicultural Magnet School
New London, Connecticut

Out beyond ideas of wrongdoing and rightdoing,
there is a field. I'll meet you there.

When the soul lies down in that grass,
the world is too full to talk about.
Ideas, language, even the phrase *each other*
doesn't make any sense.

                              —*Rumi*

Getting out of the way as a child discovers his or her world: this is my job. As a teacher, I walk a tightrope, juggling ideas and activities and expectations all the time, every day, every minute. I keep all my senses at the ready and alert as I live with children through the bit of their schooling I am responsible for, their first-grade year.

How to have a light touch; how to close my mouth before something directive comes out of it; how to listen first and suggest later, if at all: these have been my challenges while teaching five- to seven-year-olds during the past thirty years.

I watch them, and I listen listen listen—how else will I know how each unique one is growing and what he or she needs next? In my classroom there is movement, there is stillness; there is talk, there is silence; there is concentration, there is discovery. Sometimes, they sit. Sometimes, they all talk. Whatever it takes for each child to grow, dream, and learn, that is what I do.

Mary Oliver's teacher is not listening, not watching, not, I am sure, smiling. He fits well into today's disheartening devotion to assessment, routinely shoehorning his sitting and silenced square pegs into round holes. Probably he believes that the forty-five-question, computer-based math exam given every three months is good for my students.

Teachers: test, don't teach. Children: sit down, don't think or grow. When the children's "hearts are falling asleep," the heart of the teacher already has.

—Katie Johnson
Elementary School Teacher
Seattle, Washington

The Poet Dreams of the Classroom

I dreamed
I stood up in class
and I said aloud:

Teacher,
why is algebra important?

Sit down, he said.

Then I dreamed
I stood up
and I said:

Teacher, I'm weary of the turkeys
that we have to draw every fall.
May I draw a fox instead?

Sit down, he said.

Then I dreamed
I stood up once more and said:

Teacher,
my heart is falling asleep
and it wants to wake up.
It needs to be outside.

Sit down, he said.

—Mary Oliver

When I was a little boy, my weary mother, Delores Walker, would recite "Mother to Son" to me each night before I went to sleep. At the time, I wondered why I had to endure such torture. In retrospect, I realize that her feisty resolve in sharing this poem was her way of building my resilience and capacity for leadership.

As I think about my work with the Coalition of Schools Educating Boys of Color, and specifically with Sankofa Passages Program, our culturally rooted rites-of-passage program for at-risk young men, I see a link between what my mother expected of me and what the Sankofa mentors model and expect from their mentees. We ask our mentors and teachers to incorporate the poem's essential elements and imagine that all young men of color will graduate exceptionally prepared to carry and shape society's mantle, to take their rightful place in local, national, and global communities. Developing these students requires teachers to offer critical support without apology; to nurture academic as well as social and emotional growth; and to counter home, community, school, and societal stresses that often derail young men on the path to success.

The practices of *sankofa* embody the sense that "before one goes forward, one must look back." The program brings these practices to the young men we work with through the extensive use of African rites-of-passage rituals; experiential learning; and the study of African and Afro-American culture, history, and literature. For the young men on a potentially downward trajectory, our approach infuses them with resilience, determination, and a sense of a positive future. Fortunately for me, years ago, and for Sankofa mentees today, turning back is not an option. Thank you, Mom.

—Ron Walker

Founding member and Executive Director
Coalition of Schools Educating Boys of Color
Boston, Massachusetts

Mother to Son

Well, son, I'll tell you:
Life for me ain't been no crystal stair.
It's had tacks in it,
And splinters,
And boards torn up,
And places with no carpet on the floor—
Bare.
But all the time
I'se been a-climbin' on,
And reachin' landin's,
And turnin' corners,
And sometimes goin' in the dark
Where there ain't been no light.
So boy, don't you turn back.
Don't you set down on the steps
'Cause you finds it's kinder hard.
Don't you fall now—
For I'se still goin', honey,
I'se still climbin',
And life for me ain't been no crystal stair.

—*Langston Hughes*

A "ripe, flawless peach." I can feel it, taste it, savor it, deep, deep down . . . a lovely expression of what makes life wonderful. In the midst of tragedy, of the reality that life is hard and all too short, there is so much to appreciate.

When I first read this poem, it resonated with me immediately, capturing my own experiences of the process of losing my parents and my best friend to cancer. It reminded me of the unexpected graces of laughter and love and closeness that accompanied the sadness and pain. Circumstances are rarely "good" or "bad," but usually some bizarre combination of both simultaneously, and this poem's expression of these seeming contradictions continues to guide my life and work.

My work in community-based education has always focused on children living in poverty. The challenges children and families in poor communities face can be overwhelming. And yet, there are extraordinary assets in every community. Poverty refers to financial circumstances. It is easy to forget that richness in other aspects of a community may coexist with desperate need. If we do not understand and value the strengths of communities and families—friendship, history, faith, art, tradition, spirituality, love, beauty, values, creativity, happiness—and build on them, we will not be effective in our work with them.

"Otherwise" captures the hard part of life with the joy. Even faced with serious challenges, we can find the "ripe, flawless peach," but we have to look for it, and appreciate it.

—Alison Overseth
Executive Director
Partnership for After School Education
New York, New York

Otherwise

I got out of bed
on two strong legs.
It might have been
otherwise. I ate
cereal, sweet
milk, ripe, flawless
peach. It might
have been otherwise.
I took the dog uphill
to the birch wood.
All morning I did
the work I love.

At noon I lay down
with my mate. It might
have been otherwise.
We ate dinner together
at a table with silver
candlesticks. It might
have been otherwise.
I slept in a bed
in a room with paintings
on the walls, and
planned another day
just like this day.
But one day, I know,
it will be otherwise.

—*Jane Kenyon*

This is the poem I put on the first page of my dissertation. It ruthlessly reminds teachers and principals that our students are all too often a captive audience. It is the poem that inspired me to start a new school in an old, struggling city, a school where adults would have to be able to answer the question, "When are we ever going to use this?" It is the poem I use to explain to visitors at our school why we seek to throw our kids out into the world and why we strive to pull the world into their classrooms.

On a good week I have kids building fires and shelters in the woods, visiting mosques, interviewing rabbis, agitating for fair-trade chocolate, and evaluating the health and efficiencies of city buildings. At our school, we create these experiences for kids, but not just because they make better memories than "watching the clock." Done right, these experiences help students connect the skills and content they encounter in the classroom with the exigencies and opportunities they'll face in life.

Richard Brautigan's poem is the lament of far too many students who never get asked to take a genuine risk, to jump into an experience, and then to think long and hard on what they learned facing the challenge. If we are to do school right, we ought to nail this poem on the front doors of every school in the nation, and then ask ourselves, *How much time are we stealing?*

—*Stephen Mahoney*
Principal and Founder
Springfield Renaissance School
Springfield, Massachusetts

The Memoirs of Jessie James

I remember all those thousands of hours
that I spent in grade school watching the clock,
waiting for recess or lunch or to go home.
    Waiting: for anything but school.
My teachers could easily have ridden with Jesse James
    for all the time they stole from me.

—Richard Brautigan

Graduation day, June 2008. I have never felt as exhilarated as when I watched the first group of high school seniors that I counseled through the college application process walk across the graduation stage.

Bronx Lab School is a small institution founded through the Bill & Melinda Gates Foundation's small school initiative. Our students were nearly 100 percent in the free and reduced lunch program. Students zoned to the original high school graduated at a rate of 21 percent. At Bronx Lab, 92 percent of our students graduated from high school in four years. And every graduate crossed the stage with an acceptance to college. We were doing more than beating the odds, we were breaking the mold.

Although graduation from high school was an important life event for these students, having the chance to go to college was life changing. Their parents watched with pride, as they knew their child was being given an opportunity that they never had. The promise of education put their child on a different path and infused the family with a sense of possibility and hope. At the end of the ceremony, my principal read "To be of use." As I listened, I thought how odd it is that when you are submerged in a task, pulling like an ox or water buffalo, you're not fully aware of your impact; it's all about "moving things forward," doing "what has to be done, again and again." But watching these students cross that stage, I realized that I was fortunate to have found a place "to be of use" with "work that is real."

—*Amy Christie*

Network Director of College
Achievement First
New York, New York

To be of use

The people I love the best
jump into work head first
without dallying in the shallows
and swim off with sure strokes almost out of sight.
They seem to become natives of that element,
the black sleek heads of seals
bouncing like half-submerged balls.

I love people who harness themselves, an ox to a heavy cart,
who pull like water buffalo, with massive patience,
who strain in the mud and the muck to move things forward,
who do what has to be done, again and again.

I want to be with people who submerge
in the task, who go into the fields to harvest
and work in a row and pass the bags along,
who are not parlor generals and field deserters
but move in a common rhythm
when the food must come in or the fire be put out.

The work of the world is common as mud.
Botched, it smears the hands, crumbles to dust.
But the thing worth doing well done
has a shape that satisfies, clean and evident.
Greek amphoras for wine or oil,
Hopi vases that held corn, are put in museums
but you know they were made to be used.
The pitcher cries for water to carry
and a person for work that is real.

—*Marge Piercy*

For five years I worked at a "persistently failing" elementary school in West Philadelphia. More than 90 percent of my students received free or reduced lunch, and many were exposed to violence in their home and in their neighborhood. Over the years, I hardened myself to navigate the trials and tribulations associated with the violence, hopelessness, and struggles of the school community. I also discovered how my young students had to develop an inner strength to overcome the many barriers they faced on a daily basis.

One day, I received a newsletter from Teaching Tolerance in my mailbox. The newsletter had excerpts from Maya Angelou's "Still I Rise" printed on the back. The poem came just as my school was being shuttered by the district. It came after five years of battles, victories, losses, joy, pain, hope, fear, and myriad emotions, sometimes all felt in the course of one day. My colleagues and I felt like pawns in a game, being shuffled around without knowing where we might end up. We worried about our students and who would be teaching them to read, write, and do math and helping to heal their physical and emotional wounds.

The strength that the poem exudes helped me reflect on my strength as an educator and that of my students. I posted the excerpt outside my classroom in my new school. It continues to inspire me, and I hope it helps my students see this strength in themselves, that they, too, are the dream and the hope; that they, too, can rise.

—Mary Beth Hertz
Elementary Science and Technology Teacher
Philadelphia, Pennsylvania

Still I Rise

You may write me down in history
With your bitter, twisted lies,
You may trod me in the very dirt
But still, like dust, I'll rise.

Does my sassiness upset you?
Why are you beset with gloom?
'Cause I walk like I've got oil wells
Pumping in my living room.

Just like moons and like suns,
With the certainty of tides,
Just like hopes springing high,
Still I'll rise.

Did you want to see me broken?
Bowed head and lowered eyes?
Shoulders falling down like teardrops,
Weakened by my soulful cries?

Does my haughtiness offend you?
Don't you take it awful hard
'Cause I laugh like I've got gold mines
Diggin' in my own backyard.

You may shoot me with your words,
You may cut me with your eyes,
You may kill me with your hatefulness,
But still, like air, I'll rise.

Does my sexiness upset you?
Does it come as a surprise
That I dance like I've got diamonds
At the meeting of my thighs?

Out of the huts of history's shame
I rise
Up from a past that's rooted in pain
I rise
I'm a black ocean, leaping and wide,
Welling and swelling I bear in the tide.

Leaving behind nights of terror and fear
I rise
Into a daybreak that's wondrously clear
I rise
Bringing the gifts that my ancestors gave,
I am the dream and the hope of the slave.
I rise
I rise
I rise.

—Maya Angelou

Growing up in the Bronx, violence was ever present. I saw it on the news, heard it through the walls of my apartment, and felt it when gunshots exploded outside of my window. The violence that surrounded me made me so scared that in third grade, I vomited every night.

After attending boarding school and college in New England, I returned to the Bronx to teach and realized that other forms of violence plagued my community. Olive Senior's poem highlights the hidden but sinister institutional violence often endured by marginalized people and communities. It involves standardizing students and diminishing their identities in ways that silence their lives and "erase" them—a colonialism of self in the harshest sense.

Too often, we enter our classrooms focusing on our students' deficits, needs, and problems. Instead, we should focus on what they *bring* to the classroom and build on it. On the first day of school, I give my students a survey asking about them, the languages spoken at home, their academic and social strengths, and so on. I also send a letter and survey home to communicate to parents that educating their child is a collaborative effort and that I am interested in who they are and what they have to offer.

Honoring our students' lives and ensuring that there is something about them in their studies are key. Building relationships with students, their families, their community, and social justice groups enables them to feel safe, loved, and successful. Educating our children should be a collaborative responsibility, an act of solidarity.

—*Dena Simmons*

Graduate Student
Teachers College, Columbia University
New York, New York

Colonial Girls School

Borrowed images
willed our skins pale
muffled our laughter
lowered our voices
let out our hems
dekinked our hair
denied our sex in gym tunics and bloomers
harnessed our voices to madrigals
and genteel airs
yoked our minds to declensions in Latin
and the language of Shakespeare

    Told us nothing about ourselves
    There was nothing about us at all

How those pale northern eyes and
aristocratic whispers once erased us
How our loudness, our laughter
debased us

    There was nothing left of ourselves
    Nothing about us at all

Studying: *History Ancient and Modern*
Kings and Queens of England
Steppes of Russia
Wheatfields of Canada

    There was nothing of our landscape there
    Nothing about us at all

Marcus Garvey turned twice in his grave
'Thirty-eight was a beacon. A flame.
They were talking of desegregation
in Little Rock, Arkansas. Lumumba
and the Congo. To us: mumbo-jumbo.
We had read Vachal Lindsay's
vision of the jungle

    Feeling nothing about ourselves
    There was nothing about us at all

Months, years, a childhood memorising
Latin declensions
(For our language
— 'bad talking'—
detentions)

    Finding nothing about us there
    Nothing about us at all

So, friend of my childhood years
One day we'll talk about
How the mirror broke
Who kissed us awake
Who let Anansi from his bag

For isn't it strange how
northern eyes
in the brighter world before us now

Pale?

               —Olive Senior

Each day, thirty thousand students stream into hundreds of classrooms in Springfield, Massachusetts, a city that was once described as the world center of precision manufacturing. The factories are now closed, and the city struggles with joblessness and high rates of poverty.

Many of the students of Springfield come to school with the baggage, trauma, and heartache that the young poet describes. They often have been "kicked out," have been left behind, and are "looking for someone."

Each afternoon, forty of these at-risk teens come to Project Coach, a sports-based youth development program. At Project Coach, staff and students from Smith College train and prepare teens to coach, tutor, and mentor elementary school students from their own neighborhoods. These teens then run sports leagues in the local elementary schools. As coaches of young children, they must learn to deploy crucial skills in communication, conflict resolution, self-awareness, and emotional regulation. The young players look up to these teens and aspire to become coaches themselves.

My role as director of Project Coach is to embrace these teens and guide them to become powerful coaches on the field, and then support them as they work their way through high school and into college. When I am tired from working long hours or feel overwhelmed, I remember the words in this poem and the truth they carry.

The poet labels himself a "freedom writer." His poem carries all the pride and promise he feels as he tenuously grasps his new life. At Project Coach, teens with great pride embrace the label "coach" as their new role and identity.

—*Kayleigh Colombero*
Director of Project Coach
Springfield, Massachusetts

An Innocent Freedom Writer

A young black boy filled with innocence and care,
looking for someone, but no one is there.
His first day of school, the father's not around,
to comfort his son when he's sad and down.
Looks up to his brother who knows money and power,
watching his back every single hour.
An innocent boy is now twelve years of age,
and finds himself locked up in a human-sized cage.
An innocent young man is now a criminal mind,
having nightmares of murders every single time.
But this time you'll think this fool should see the light,
but he's jumped in a gang and they nickname him "Snipe."
Kicked out of the house and left in the cold.
Have you been through this at eleven years old?
He says to himself "no one cares for me,"
then makes his bed in an old park tree.
The next time a park bench, how long can it last?
Will he forget this dreadful, dreadful past!
He goes to Wilson High with a messed-up trail,
and meets a guardian angel named Erin Gruwell.
He learns about the Holocaust, Anne Frank and the Jews.
Now the time comes that he should choose.
He meets Anna, Terri, Tommy, and others.
These are the innocent boy's new sisters and brothers.

A 0.5 now a 2.8—
Change is good, for those that wait.
He's back to innocence, but still has fear,
that death is upon him and drawing near.
But people say it's hard to see,
this life of emotions is all about me.
All this is true, because I'm not a liar
just a brokenhearted male with a label—Freedom Writer!

—*The Freedom Writers with Erin Gruwell*

Moment to Moment

Schools, as in all of modern life, struggle against an epidemic of busyness. The pace of life in schools has greatly intensified as educators work to keep up with electronic communication, meet new assessment regulations, and implement various new reform initiatives. The toll of being always flat-out busy exacts a cost in myriad ways, including a general sense of fatigue and a feeling that teaching provides little opportunity to achieve a healthy work-life balance.

The contributors in this section describe how this freneticism can make it difficult for them to do their best and most inspired work. They acknowledge the swirl of demands facing them but resist defaulting to thoughtless patterns devoid of their highest ideals. Instead, they devise routines, construct patterns, and embrace alternative ways of being that provide time to think, to learn, to catch their breath, and to take stock.

These educators understand how in a realm where showing up requires vast reserves of emotional intelligence, ongoing reflection, and creative problem solving, they need to take care of themselves and each other. They turn to poems, contemplative practices, and colleagues to help them teach with a full heart and a clearer mind. They recognize, as Herman Hesse describes in his poem, that wisdom comes from resisting the prevailing pace: "The river has / taught me to listen; you will learn from / it too."

In recent years I have struggled, not with the biology standards I teach, but with the expectation that every moment of every class will be prescheduled by the first day of the school year, that we will all follow the same course and successfully arrive at our destination at exactly the same moment. The pace and demands of this journey have intensified with more furlough days, more testing, and less learning.

It's easy in this climate to avoid creativity, abandon flexibility, and take all of the joy out of teaching and learning. Inspiration came unexpectedly one morning, when my yoga teacher read "Advice" by Bill Holm. "Advice" speaks to me of the craze for mandated rhythms of teaching (the "'Do-Your-Work' in 4/4 time") and of the frustrations that come when things are too metered, too planned (the "'What-Do-You-Expect' waltz").

Somehow that woman with black eyes gives me hope. I keep this poem posted above my sink at school, and I read it every time I make a cup of tea, do dishes, or wash my hands. It helps me remember that my students and I occasionally need the jumpy rhythms. We need the freedom to take an unexpected detour, explore our collective interests, be creative, take a chance. And we also need to return to 4/4 time, until it's time to dance with the black-eyed lady again. When the standards-based nature of education feels crushing in its uniformity, "Advice" gives me permission to embrace my creativity in the classroom.

—Teri O'Donnell

High School Biology Teacher
Santa Rosa, California

Advice

Someone dancing inside us
has learned only a few steps:
the "Do-Your-Work" in 4/4 time,
and the "What-Do-You-Expect" waltz.
He hasn't noticed yet the woman
standing away from the lamp,
the one with black eyes
who knows the rumba
and strange steps in jumpy
rhythms from the mountains of Bulgaria.
If they dance together,
something unexpected will happen.
If they don't, the next world
will be a lot like this one.

—Bill Holm

Somehow, like an oracle, Katha Pollitt knew that my storm had come. There, in the September 22, 2003, issue of the *New Yorker*, Pollitt had planted for my discovery a gut-punch of a poem, "Lilacs in September." I was one week away from the beginning of autumn quarter classes, initiating my fifth year of lecturer purgatory. My marriage had just collapsed, traumatizing me and our two children, and I felt untethered and purposeless. And then, in exactly the right place and at precisely the right time, Pollitt's poem slapped me awake. The poem opens with a wallop:

> Shocked to the root
> like the lilac bush
> in the vacant lot
> by the hurricane—

"Shocked," indeed. This bold, staccato word opens that first stanza, and Pollitt ends the stanza with a *hurricane*, for heaven's sake.

But it's the last three lines of the fourth and concluding stanza that I return to repeatedly. The out-of-season lilac blossoms seem to ask: "*What will unleash / itself in you / when your storm comes?*"

Hanging on the bulletin board at work and at home, the poem reminds me daily that the "wind or rain" in our lives brings moments of startling insight and beauty. Trauma can hurt, but, like lightning, it can release unexpected wonders. Sent in new directions, I developed new friends, began appreciating my children's mother in a new light, landed a rewarding administrative position at work, and took up the blues harmonica. Now, rereading the poem every September prepares me spiritually for whatever maelstrom is heading for my shore, and for whatever it will unleash in me.

—*David S. Goldstein*

Director
UW Bothell Teaching and Learning Center
Bothell, Washington

Lilacs in September

Shocked to the root
like the lilac bush
in the vacant lot
by the hurricane—

whose black branch split
by wind or rain
has broken out
unseasonably

into these scant ash-
colored blossoms
lifted high
as if to say

to passersby
What will unleash
itself in you
when your storm comes?

> —Katha Pollitt

In some ways as a leader I am called to be the ferryman for others, to help them cross what may seem like insurmountable challenges. I must not only listen to the river but help others see the challenges not as obstacles, but as a means of journeying forward to new and better ways of thinking about schools, students, and our own passion for teaching and leading.

I crossed my own river when I became a superintendent, a job I never aspired to, but one I was called to as I made the crossing from the business world back to education. In my first year we had to cut our budget by 10 percent. The next year, state directives included the effective dissolution of teachers' unions, a mandated teacher evaluation system, and significantly increased student performance standards.

The river was rough. Many clung to the shore hoping that things would go back to the way they were. A few courageous teachers and administrators saw opportunities for innovation and used their agency and voice to make things happen despite deep and sometimes harsh resistance from their colleagues and despite being pummeled by the legislature and conservative media.

We still hit a few rocks, some quite large, but by listening to the river, we were able to create new efforts, such as multi-age options for elementary school students, student support periods, and a new teacher mentor program, just to name a few. Each of these things is relatively small, but the fact that they happened at all in the current climate is a true crossing.

—Rachel Boechler

Superintendent
Fox Point-Bayside Schools
Milwaukee, Wisconsin

The Ferryman

I
am
only a
ferryman
and it is my
task to take people
across and to all
of them my river
has been nothing but a
hindrance on their journey.
They have traveled for money
and business, to weddings and
on pilgrimages; the river has been
in their way and the ferryman was
there to take them quickly
across the obstacle. However,
Amongst the thousands there have been a few,
four or five, to whom the river was not an
obstacle. They heard its voice and listened
to it, and the river has become holy
to them, as it has to me. The river has
taught me to listen; you will learn from
it too. The river knows everything;
one can learn everything from it.

—*Herman Hesse*

This poem helps me when my usual way of approaching an idea or a subject isn't working. But it is my greatest guide when something unexpected happens, when someone asks a question that causes me to stray from "the edge of all our plans" and into territory for which I have not prepared.

A few years back, I received an email stating that it was important for the reputation of our highly competitive graduate programs to be tough on grades and class attendance. I was particularly aware of being a "softie" in a world that wants hard edges, rules, and toughness. And so I told my graduate leadership class that attendance was mandatory. No excuses.

During the second class, Caroline said she had a dilemma. She'd been asked to represent the Air Force as its runner in an important race. But she would only compete if I said it was okay to miss the class. All eyes were on me. I asked, "Do you really want to run it?" Her eyes lit up. "Yes," was her quiet answer.

Caroline won that race and went on to win many others. That day, that moment, when I bent my own world-imposed rule because of the look in her eyes, has stayed with me.

External mandates increasingly encroach on our classrooms and challenge our teacher's judgment—I strive to keep alive and strong that part of teaching that is all about knowing what makes the heart sing and being open to "the appointments we were born to keep."

—*Judy Sorum Brown*
Leadership Faculty
College Park, Maryland

The Appointment

What if, on the first sunny day,
on your way to work, a colorful bird
sweeps in front of you down a
street you've never heard of.

You might pause and smile,
a sweet beginning to your day.

Or you might step into that street
and realize there are many ways to work.

You might sense the bird knows some-
thing you don't and wander after.

You might hesitate when the bird
turns down an alley. For now
there is a tension: Is what the
bird knows worth being late?

You might go another block or two,
thinking you can have it both ways.
But soon you arrive at the edge
of all your plans.

The bird circles back for you
and you must decide which
appointment you were
born to keep.

—*Mark Nepo*

A theme running through my leadership career working with adults, both parents and professional educators, has come from my decades-long practice of yoga. There is a saying in yoga—"Don't sacrifice the breath for the pose." It's not about looking good or being good looking, it's about breathing in a comfortable space, which then eventually can catapult and liberate you into being ready for "the pose" or the "next pose," or the next level of poses.

What I have drawn from this is to keep things simple, breathe, and focus on grounding yourself in whatever the dynamics are that need your attention.

As a principal, you are expected to have a five-year plan to move a school forward, and a ten-year "vision," but first you need a great ten-minute plan because the life of a principal needs to be artfully and authentically compartmentalized.

No one wants to hear about the last problem you handled, or see your eyes wandering down the hall, or witness you checking your iPhone when he or she needs you to listen to and show empathy toward his or her issue. Take the time to look into people's eyes, and be immersed in the energy of the moment. Don't be distracted, become technology-temptation-proof.

The life of a principal can be one long string of interruptions if your approach is not "in the present" and not focused. In the end, you must ask yourself: *What will be my "footprints"? As a result of my leadership, did I leave the school a better place than it was when I found it?*

—Sandi Bisceglia
Executive Director
International Network of Principals' Centers
Islamorada, Florida

Footprints by the Sea

Our hearts listened awhile to the dying sea,
and the cry of gulls lost in the wind;
then we spoke of life, and hope, and love,
and the price of giving in:

of how great battles might be won,
how daring deeds are daring done,
how magic moments slip away,
like love, and at what cost;

of ancient struggles, near forgot—
the ghosts of once-bright Camelot—
of tears and treasures left behind,
deep footprints by the sea . . .

—*Captain Ed Davidson*

Many years ago, I attended a celebration honoring an old friend on the eve of his retirement after a distinguished forty-year career as a school leader. I was a brand-new school leader struggling with the ebbs and flows of my new role, and I remember eagerly anticipating his response when somebody asked him to detail the most important lesson he learned during his tenure. He paused and then said, "A good school learns somehow to bend itself around the strengths and weaknesses of its leader." Huh?! I was baffled.

Decisiveness, strength, vision. These were my gods! Uncertainty, fear, failure? How could these, well, *imperfection*s be integral leadership elements in the growth of a school?

But now as I approach my own retirement, having spent many years teaching leadership, I am reminded once again of my friend's advice—echoed in the essential paradox of "The Guest House." We must, as Rumi says, "welcome and entertain them all," our strengths and our weaknesses, understanding all of them as necessary to our own development and, ultimately, the life of a school. To better practice leadership, we must "be grateful" in accepting these challenges.

And today, when asked a similar question by a young leader, I say: "Let others really know you; learn to fall gracefully when you tumble; and, above all, be vulnerable." These are the surest ways I know to foster trusting relationships, genuine achievement, and the blessings of a conscious leadership life.

—Richard H. Ackerman

College Professor of Educational Leadership
Brooksville, Maine

The Guest House

This being human is a guest house.
Every morning a new arrival.

A joy, a depression, a meanness,
some momentary awareness comes
as an unexpected visitor.

Welcome and entertain them all!
Even if they're a crowd of sorrows,
who violently sweep your house
empty of its furniture,
still, treat each guest honorably.
He may be clearing you out
for some new delight.

The dark thought, the shame, the malice,
meet them at the door laughing,
and invite them in.

Be grateful for whoever comes,
because each has been sent
as a guide from beyond.

—Rumi

As a superintendent, I consider my to-do list to be my constant companion. It helps keep me focused. It prioritizes my daily activities. It gives me a sense of achievement when I cross off completed tasks. The one thing it doesn't accomplish is to just let me be . . . after all, it's a to-do list, not a to-be list!

We all seem to be addicted to the demands placed on us by ourselves and others. Finding ways to escape the busyness in our lives requires thoughtful consideration. I make every effort to get away from my work environment for short periods of time. I may take a solitary lunch or a drive around a country block. Doing so changes my perspective and gives me the valuable "alone time" I need to reframe my thinking and keep myself in touch with my inner voice.

I've extended this belief in designing the agendas for our monthly Leadership Team meetings. We incorporate an element of self-reflection into each meeting, which helps bring us to that space and serves to strengthen the personal relationships that are vital to our success.

"Flight from the Shadow" is the perfect antidote to the frantic pace of everyday life. It reminds me and other district leaders that we must step into the shade, sit down, and stay still. Being still, even for brief periods of time, gives us the chance to listen to our inner voice, gain broader perspectives, and thus better serve ourselves as well as our students and staff.

—*Mark Bielang*
Superintendent
Paw Paw Public Schools
Paw Paw, Michigan

Flight from the Shadow

There was a man who was so disturbed by the sight of his own shadow and so displeased with his own footsteps that he determined to get rid of both. The method he hit upon was to run away from them.

So he got up and ran. But every time he put his foot down there was another step, while his shadow kept up with him without the slightest difficulty.

He attributed his failure to the fact that he was not running fast enough. So he ran faster and faster, without stopping, until he finally dropped dead.

He failed to realize that if he merely stepped into the shade, his shadow would vanish, and if he sat down and stayed still, there would be no more footsteps.

—Chuang Tzu

For two years I was privileged to work for our state's department of education. I was charged with helping teachers and administrators increase student achievement based on assessment scores. I accumulated many miles on my car—and more on my psyche—attempting to apply temporary bandages to wounds of school culture that ultimately begged further treatment and healing time.

While on the road, I developed a bad habit of escaping by sleeping in headphones, plunging myself into fitful sleeps by drowning out my own inner silence that contradicted my daily work.

Exhausted, I left the state department and became an administrator in a local school district. In a district meeting, I expressed gratitude to be off the road, but also a lingering restlessness—a discontent and disconnect between my ideal of school reform and its red-tape realities. In response, one of my new colleagues (who would become my best friend) introduced me to Thomas Merton's work and the idea to "be still" and "listen to the stones of the wall." Merton wrote words for which my soul had been searching.

So much reform practice has become focused on adhering to mandates and securing speedy compliance that it feels like "the whole world is secretly on fire." Since encountering Merton, in my work as an administrator, and now as a workshop facilitator and a university professor, I encourage reflection, silence, communication, and taking the time necessary to effect deep, meaningful change.

From that first meeting, Merton's philosophy began to inform my work and my life. It still does.

—Thomas A. Stewart
College Professor of Education
Bowling Green, Kentucky

In Silence

Be still
Listen to the stones of the wall.
Be silent, they try
To speak your

Name.
Listen
To the living walls.
Who are you?
Who
Are you? Whose
Silence are you?

Who (be quiet)
Are you (as these stones
Are quiet). Do not
Think of what you are
Still less of
What you may one day be.
Rather
Be what you are (but who?) be
The unthinkable one
You do not know.

O be still, while
You are still alive,
And all things live around you
Speaking (I do not hear)
To your own being,
Speaking by the Unknown
That is in you and in themselves.

"I will try, like them
To be my own silence:
And this is difficult. The whole
World is secretly on fire. The stones
Burn, even the stones
They burn me. How can a man be still or
Listen to all things burning? How can he dare
To sit with them when
All their silence
Is on fire?"

—*Thomas Merton*

Too often, we leave the essence of who we are in search of power and energy. We take the bait and follow the signs that society sets up for us. We bend and tuck and pretend in order to meet the definition of who they *think* we are. We do a helluva job at it. We go days, weeks, years convinced that this is who we really are.

And then, one day, whether through a tragedy, a divorce, a heartbreak, or a sense of impending burnout, we seek to make a change. Faced with an overload of work, I turned to mindfulness meditation and discovered that monitoring how we pay attention and what we pay attention to can lead to significant changes in our lives. We can reclaim our true power and, as Derek Walcott states, arrive at our "own door." We can peel the stranger from the mirror, and our reflection becomes our truest self, the divinity that lies inside of us.

If we all operated from this source, this awareness, we could shift from a country that operates from fear to one that operates from love. To this end, as a Congressman, I proposed the Academic, Social, and Emotional Learning Act of 2011 to fund initiatives that help children learn the personal competencies that Walcott describes as core to a loving life: self-awareness, self-management, and responsible decision making.

We do not have to look outward for love. It is right here. Wherever we are. Search no more.

—Tim Ryan
Congressman
Ohio Thirteenth Congressional District
Howland, Ohio

Love After Love

The time will come
when, with elation,
you will greet yourself arriving
at your own door, in your own mirror,
and each will smile at the other's welcome,

and say, sit here. Eat.
You will love again the stranger who was your self.
Give wine. Give bread. Give back your heart
to itself, to the stranger who has loved you

all your life, whom you ignored
for another, who knows you by heart.
Take down the love letters from the bookshelf,

the photographs, the desperate notes,
peel your own image from the mirror.
Sit. Feast on your life.

—Derek Walcott

Together

Despite being around others nearly all the time, teachers ironically feel a tremendous sense of isolation. They work with children and students in crowded and intensely busy spaces, yet they have little routine interaction with other adults. The scarcity of ongoing exchanges with colleagues creates a culture in which teachers "go it alone" and develop habits of self-reliance.

But teaching as a private endeavor can contribute to feeling powerless and vulnerable to criticism by parents, students, and administrators. This sense has intensified as states and municipalities have embraced evaluation systems that include the public release of standardized test score data from teachers' classrooms.

The teachers in this section lift their voice in resistance to the norms of isolation. They contend that to be cut off from peers and colleagues is to be diminished in both one's spirit and one's practice. Through these poems and commentaries, they explore the emotions and sensitivities that arise when teachers reflect on and then work to disrupt the patterns of isolation that hold sway in teaching. They describe how they are most alive and resilient when they feel connected to others. This is true both in encountering the normal day-to-day challenges of teaching and when they are overwhelmed by the grief that children and adults sometimes face.

For almost forty years, I have walked into unlikely classrooms that aren't mine for long. I began my career teaching elementary and middle school students in the public schools. But when my husband died and our children were young, I fell into the role of an adjunct writing and resource instructor.

Since then, I have taught in elementary, middle, and high schools; English as a second language classrooms; art schools; colleges; community colleges; and jails. I have taught in heated and unheated rooms, in dance studios and old equipment closets. Whatever the setting, I have to be ready to quickly create a safe environment for students, a place where our lives will briefly interact. Every time I turn the doorknob (or get buzzed in at the jail), I pause and ask for the ability to teach this group, these students, in the way they need so that the lessons and learning can be carried away and used long after we part.

It is temporary, sometimes lonely work. Most often, I work in isolation, not knowing my colleagues or staff. John Daniel's poem makes me feel a part of a tribe, of something larger. It helps me understand that this group, this day, this lesson is the only one. If I leave having accomplished the "gift of good work," it is enough for me and the students I teach. My copy of this poem is in my wallet, the paper worn thin. I find it is useful not only for teaching but also for beginning every day.

—*Melissa Madenski*

Middle School Writing Teacher
Neskowin, Oregon

A Prayer among Friends

Among other wonders of our lives, we are alive
with one another, we walk here
in the light of this unlikely world
that isn't ours for long.
May we spend generously
the time we are given.
May we enact our responsibilities
as thoroughly as we enjoy
our pleasures. May we see with clarity,
may we seek a vision
that serves all beings, may we honor
the mystery surpassing our sight,
and may we hold in our hands
the gift of good work
and bear it forth whole, as we
were borne forth by a power we praise
to this one Earth, this homeland of all we love.

—*John Daniel*

As an introvert, I would be content to stay in my office, close the door, eat my lunch at my desk, and interact as little as possible with colleagues. And as a faculty member of color at a private university, maintaining a certain level of detachment can feel like the emotionally safe thing to do.

But although quiet and solitude feel comfortable to me, I know that shutting myself away is not an option; so, I take several deep breaths and venture out. And each time I go to the cafeteria for lunch or participate in faculty meetings and on committees, I am richly blessed in one way or another.

My time with students affects me in the same way. I am energized by their youth and find great pleasure in taking the time to mentor them in any way I can. I frequently remind students that there is no shame in asking for and accepting academic assistance. We all need someone at different places in our lives—no one of us "can make it out here alone." I also remind them that when we are not as needy, we should take the time to give back to those who are.

Maya Angelou's writings seem to be those of a dear friend as she conveys a sensitive understanding of the life journey we are all experiencing. My brown, fragile, 1970s paperback edition of her poems is my constant companion, and ensures that I am never really alone.

—Nina Ashur

College Professor and Director
Learning Enrichment Center
Azusa, California

Alone

Lying, thinking
Last night
How to find my soul a home
Where water is not thirsty
And bread loaf is not stone
I came up with one thing
And I don't believe I'm wrong
That nobody,
But nobody
Can make it out here alone.

Alone, all alone
Nobody, but nobody
Can make it out here alone.

There are some millionaires
With money they can't use
Their wives run round like banshees
Their children sing the blues
They've got expensive doctors
To cure their hearts of stone.
But nobody
No, nobody
Can make it out here alone.

Alone, all alone
Nobody, but nobody
Can make it out here alone.

Now if you listen closely
I'll tell you what I know
Storm clouds are gathering
The wind is gonna blow
The race of man is suffering
And I can hear the moan,
'Cause nobody,
But nobody
Can make it out here alone.

Alone, all alone
Nobody, but nobody
Can make it out here alone.

—*Maya Angelou*

So many of us see our classroom the way Stephen Dunn sees his car in this poem. We enter our "sacred place," start our engine, "play the things we've chosen," and are off on our beautiful drive. We have an amazing job that lets us travel that way.

Frustration with flavor-of-the-day reforms helps fuel these independent adventures. Adopting a "this too shall pass" attitude, we drive far from regulations that cramp our autonomy and innovation.

Yet, there are costs associated with these isolated journeys. If as teachers we are driving in different directions, how do we know that all the destinations are worthwhile? And driving alone, we miss the new ideas and camaraderie that come when we talk about what we have learned and push each other to think about the decisions we are making.

A math teacher I interviewed for my dissertation summed up this tension perfectly: "We all want to do it our way, even if we have no evidence that it works. Before [we started doing more collaborative work], we would've said, 'Here's the test,' and gone with it. 'The kid got a bad grade? Oh well.' There would have been no discussion about whether there were bad questions or evaluation of ourselves as teachers."

As teachers, we need the space to be creative and innovative, but when we work collaboratively and with common purpose, we improve our craft and better serve our students. Much of the focus of my work these days is on trying to help teachers find that balance.

—*Dan Mindich*

High School Teacher and Administrator
Honolulu, Hawai'i

The Sacred

After the teacher asked if anyone had
   a sacred place
and the students fidgeted and shrank

in their chairs, the most serious of them all
   said it was his car,
being in it alone, his tape deck playing

things he'd chosen, and others knew the truth
   had been spoken
and began speaking about their rooms,

their hiding places, but the car kept coming up,
   the car in motion,
music filling it, and sometimes one other person

who understood the bright altar of the dashboard
   and how far away
a car could take him from the need

to speak, or to answer, the key
   in having a key
and putting it in, and going.

                  —*Stephen Dunn*

Of all of the challenges I imagined I would face in launching a network of charter schools, the one I least considered was having to fire a teacher. We intentionally devised a rigorous screening process and provided our teachers with ongoing professional development. With these structures in place, I assumed that we would have a culture that was free from the worries of "letting someone go." Despite our best efforts, I have at times had to make that difficult decision, knowing that our students deserve passionate and committed teachers who can work together as a team.

In carrying this out, I have typically faced three kinds of teachers. First, there were the frustrated teachers who had unrealistic expectations of what it means to teach in a school that focuses on "at-risk" students. Then there were those teachers with clear evidence of misconduct, frequent absences, or a lack of professionalism. And finally there were those who were in the wrong position, maybe even the wrong profession. The math teacher who really wanted to write science fiction novels. The guidance counselor who dreamed of being a singer. When the dream grows greater than a teacher's day job, and performance is affected, it's time to move on.

Though James A. Autry's poem references the firing of a salesman, many of his lines ring true in relation to my own experience. The poem comforts me, letting me know I am not the only one who has had to put in motion this painful process. It reminds me that everyone—including the one doing the firing—needs to be treated with respect and compassion.

—*Brian Dixon*
Founder
Mentorship Academy
Baton Rouge, Louisiana

On Firing A Salesman

It's like a little murder,
taking his life,
his reason for getting on the train,
his lunches at fancy restaurants,
and his meetings in warm and sunny places
where they all gather,
these smiling men,
in sherbet slacks and blue blazers,
and talk about business
but never about prices,
never breaking the law
about the prices they charge.

But what about the prices they pay?
What about gray evenings in the bar car
and smoke-filled clothes and hair
and children already asleep
and wives who say
"you stink"
when they come to bed?
What about the promotions they don't get,
the good accounts they lose
to some kid MBA
because somebody up there
thinks their energy is gone?

What about those times they see in a mirror
or the corner of their eye
some guy at the club shake his head
when they walk through the locker room
the way they shook their heads years ago
at an old duffer
whose handicap had grown along with his age?

And what about this morning,
the summons,
the closed door,
and somebody shaved and barbered and shined
fifteen years their junior
trying to put on a sad face
and saying he understands?

A murder with no funeral,
nothing but those quick steps outside the door,
those set jaws,
those confident smiles,
that young disregard for even the thought
of a salesman's mortality.

—James A. Autry

As a child, I saw the direct impact my mother had as a teacher. She inspired her students. She helped change their lives, and they often came back to see her or would write to tell her so. I was in awe of the impact she had on them.

I yearned to have that type of impact on the world.

Flash forward a decade. As a college student, I saw *Dead Poet's Society* starring Robin Williams. I was mesmerized. I loved how he inspired his students to think for themselves, be passionate learners, and challenge the status quo. I can still close my eyes and hear him talking about Robert Herrick's poem and exhorting his students to imagine the impact they might have on the world: "Did [these former students] wait until it was too late to make from their lives even one iota of what they were capable? . . . Carpe diem, seize the day, boys, make your lives extraordinary."[1]

Was I going to go through life without making an impact? Certainly not!

Every August I watch *Dead Poet's Society* to ground and motivate me for the challenges I will face during the upcoming school year, asking myself: *What will my impact be on this year? How can I best help the children and the teachers in my school? How can I help change the world each and every day, knowing that tomorrow I might be gone?*

Carpe diem is my mantra. For almost twenty-five years, this poem has shaped me and pushed me to be my very best for my students, my staff, and my family.

—Cordell Jones

Principal
Alamo Heights Junior School
San Antonio, Texas

---

1. *"Carpe Diem." Dead Poets Society*, directed by Peter Weir (Burbank, CA: Walt Disney Studios, 1989), film.

To the Virgins, to make much of Time

Gather ye Rose-buds while ye may,
   Old Time is still a flying:
And this same flower that smiles today,
   To-morrow will be dying.

The glorious Lamp of Heaven, the Sun,
   The higher he's a getting;
The sooner will his Race be run,
   And neerer he's to Setting.

That Age is best, which is the first,
   When Youth and Blood are warmer;
But being spent, the worse, and worst
   Times, still succeed the former.

Then be not coy, but use your time;
   And while ye may, goe marry:
For having lost but once your prime,
   You may for ever tarry.

—*Robert Herrick*

I have heard this poem read at graduations and memorials—significant moments of transition and transformation. It is also imprinted on the wall leading to the dining hall at St. Mary's College of Maryland—a school that I know well because my husband taught there, as did Lucille Clifton.

Often, when I recite these lines aloud, "may the tide . . . carry you out beyond the face of fear," I think about my own fear of using my voice with agency. In a profession caught in a storm of external solutions, I have learned that I can do my best and most meaningful work when my colleagues and I seek together new ways to "sail through this to that," and find true north for ourselves and our students.

After thirty years in education, I undertook my most ambitious challenge and cofounded the Chesapeake Public Charter School—which is the first charter school in our region. During the four-year planning process, which was filled with uncertainties and roadblocks, a growing circle of parents and teachers shared leadership. As the initiator of this venture that often felt like sailing against the "tide," I frequently felt the immensity of the task.

By carefully listening to each other, we formed a community of trusting relationships that could carry us "beyond the face of fear" as we confronted rejection, an appeals process, and numerous logistical and financial obstacles. Together we created a safe space for what has become a thriving community of learners and leaders.

—Kathleen Glaser
Co-founder
Chesapeake Public Charter School
St. Mary's City, Maryland

blessing the boats

(at St. Mary's)

may the tide
that is entering even now
the lip of our understanding
carry you out
beyond the face of fear
may you kiss
the wind then turn from it
certain that it will
love your back   may you
open your eyes to water
water waving forever
and may you in your innocence
sail through this to that

—*Lucille Clifton*

There is beauty in the open doors of a community college. Beauty, hope, potential, and promise for an entire community: university-bound students entering honors programs, immigrants learning English, bricklayers studying construction management, grandparents tackling new technologies.

Since 2009 I have made a practice of sharing a poem with my colleagues at the end of each week of classes. I include some comments about how I think the poem speaks to our work together. As soon as I read "Happiness," I knew I wanted to begin the fall semester with it. The image of those two boys reminded me of the way prospective students often come in pairs—perhaps sharing the excitement, perhaps supporting each other, as they step into a new phase of their lives. The mother accompanying her undocumented teenage daughter to hear for herself that the Maryland DREAM law[2] will at last give her child a brighter future. The two young men, gradually shedding earbuds, shades, and hoodies, as they come in to talk about their plans.

Yes, all summer long we see the two boys in this poem: people coming to us because they have decided to go somewhere with their lives. People in that existential moment when they step through our doors, full of anticipation—happy because something has just begun.

What we do, obviously, is much more complex than dispensing happiness, and goodness knows the happiness part can be fleeting. But it's very real, that happiness, and to paraphrase Raymond Carver, it goes beyond, really, any early-semester talk about it.

—Dennis Huffman

Program Director
Prince George's Community College
Hyattsville, Maryland

---

2. In 2013 Maryland began allowing qualified undocumented students to pay in-state tuition at community colleges.

Happiness

So early it's still almost dark out.
I'm near the window with coffee,
and the usual early morning stuff
that passes for thought.
When I see the boy and his friend
walking up the road
to deliver the newspaper.
They wear caps and sweaters,
and one boy has a bag over his shoulder.
They are so happy
they aren't saying anything, these boys.
I think if they could, they would take
each other's arm.
It's early in the morning,
and they are doing this thing together.
They come on, slowly.
The sky is taking on light,
though the moon still hangs pale over the water.
Such beauty that for a minute
death and ambition, even love,
doesn't enter into this.
Happiness. It comes on
unexpectedly. And goes beyond, really,
any early morning talk about it.

—*Raymond Carver*

Close to one hundred educators were gathered for the second day of a two-day workshop when news of the shootings at Sandy Hook Elementary began to move through the crowd. Once in a while, a large group shares a powerful emotional reaction to an event. Kennedy, King, Columbine, 9/11—this was like that.

We had started that morning learning about a traditional Maasai greeting and response: "How are the children?" "The children are well!" We loved that, with all that it said about communities that nurture and support children. That simple greeting reminded us of why we were there, working to make our schools better places for children.

When the news came, we suddenly knew that the children were not well. We were disconsolate. We simply could not find a way to comfort ourselves.

That night, a poem came to my mind. This is it. I'm not sure I can explain why it brought me comfort, but it did. And does.

—Kenneth Rocke
Director
Pioneer Valley District and School Assistance Center
Heath, Massachusetts

Little Elegy

for a child who skipped rope

Here lies resting, out of breath,
Out of turns, Elizabeth
Whose quicksilver toes not quite
Cleared the whirring edge of night.

Earth whose circles round us skim
Till they catch the lightest limb,
Shelter now Elizabeth
And for her sake trip up Death.

—X. J. Kennedy

One of the most important responsibilities of my job as the president and CEO of the NEA Foundation is fostering the collaborative efforts of public school educators, their unions, school districts, and communities to develop learning conditions that support and improve student performance.

Much of this work involves procedures, systems, and negotiations over contracts and administrative structures, but no matter how legalistic the work, I hold on to what I learned when I taught school in Albany, New York, where I grew up. There is one common trait that is in the DNA of teachers—a stubborn and intense desire to do everything possible to help their students flourish and succeed.

When I found this poem buried in the *New York Times*, just a few weeks before the NEA Foundation's awards gala, I knew I needed to share it with the more than eight hundred attendees to honor the bond that is at the heart of great teaching.

Over the past year, the national debate on teacher evaluation and student assessment has been intense. And although these conversations are critical to systemic reform, what is often lost is the understanding and acknowledgment of the silent and persistent focus that teachers have on "their kids." Mel Glenn's poem and the heroism of teachers during the Newtown, Connecticut tragedy remind us to stay humble: teachers are bound to "their kids" through sacred contracts "forged in love" that go above and beyond the legalese.

—Harriet Sanford

President and CEO
NEA Foundation
Washington, DC

A Teacher's Contract

Between the teachers and the city
there exists a contract,
full of legal obligations on both sides,
pay steps, duties and responsibilities,
all to be negotiated.
But there is a higher, more important contract,
that requires no lawyers,
no arbitration, no picket lines.
It is a contract given, not stated,
ironclad and universal.
It is written on the smart board,
demonstrated in the halls, surrounding
student desks and classroom walls.
It is a contract automatically renewed each year,
forged in love, witnessed daily.
It is never up for a discussion or vote.
It is unchangeable, immutable.
And in Newtown the contract
remains, unbroken in life, in death,
consisting of only two words:
"My kids."

—*Mel Glenn*

Called to Teach

*W*ork is a serious and meaningful matter. What we do and how we understand the impact of our work shape our sense of identity and our self-worth. Teachers describe being drawn to teaching by a passion for students, a love of subject matter, and an abiding belief that the work of teaching involves connecting students to powerful ideas and promising futures. Teaching promised a life well lived: a life of purpose, meaning, and dignity.

Perhaps because teachers yearn to make a difference and come to the work devoted to the ideals of service and justice, they also struggle mightily with self-doubt and a sense of being unable to meet the expectations they have for themselves. Teachers contend with the bad days, the long stretches of a year when things feel in disarray, and the times of a career when they feel disenchanted by the overwhelming pressure and they question their choice of profession.

The poet Wendell Berry wrote, "we have come to our real work." With "real" he refers to the beauty of important work done well and the heartbreak of important work that is beyond what one can accomplish. This paradox is the heart and soul, the wonder and burden, of the teaching life. The stories in this section, and throughout the entire book, speak to this tension—and to why so many teachers choose to stay, despite all the challenges, in this noble profession.

This poem always brings me back to why I became a teacher. I must've been around twenty years old and was doing some volunteer child care. I remember a five-year-old boy excitedly showing me an insect he'd found, and can see that younger version of myself crouching down next to him to peer into the grass. I remember feeling exhilarated to witness his discovery and listen to his observations, which inspired me to pursue teaching.

Of course, there were other reasons as well. I wanted to share the incredible privileges I was experiencing as a first-generation college student. I wanted to bring opportunities for exploration and engagement to students who might not otherwise get to learn in this way.

In the sixteen years since, the road has not been easy. The pressures of testing and standardization increase each passing year. Yet, I continue to find ways to inspire my students. From starting a creative writing group in Mississippi to welcoming a fairy to live in my classroom in the Bronx, I try to embrace the paradox and create different types of learning spaces within more traditional frameworks.

As Gary Snyder advises, I work hard to *stay together* with my students and build the strong relationships that are the foundation for all else. I work to create those moments for discovery—to *learn the flowers*, or the insects, or the birds. To *go light* and not let the weight of the system take my energy away from what I know is best—for the children.

—Julia Hill
Reading Specialist
St. Paul, Minnesota

For the Children

The rising hills, the slopes,
of statistics
lie before us.
the steep climb
of everything, going up,
up, as we all
go down.

In the next century
or the one beyond that,
they say,
are valleys, pastures,
we can meet there in peace
if we make it.

To climb these coming crests
one word to you, to
you and your children:

stay together
learn the flowers
go light

—*Gary Snyder*

In 2004 I left corporate America and the promise of great earnings to become a professional educator.

I applied to and was accepted into an alternative preparation program sponsored by Atlanta Public Schools. The other career changers and I had six weeks to learn how to become teachers. We learned how to write lesson and unit plans, manage a classroom, and interact with parents. We also learned that working in an inner-city school district was not going to be easy.

In 2005 I began teaching sixth-grade mathematics at Henry M. Turner Middle School. It was trial by fire. I came to work early and stayed late. On weekends, I graded papers and planned lessons. I even dreamed about my students. Teaching became my life. It consumed me, and I struggled.

I struggled to make my classes interesting, my lessons engaging, and my examples relevant to my students' lives. I was baited into petty squabbles with twelve- and thirteen-year-olds. I chose my battles poorly and lost far more often than I won. I hated how my struggles made me feel, but I endured knowing I could, and would, become a better teacher.

I laughed the first time I read Maya Angelou's poem. It begins, "I keep on dying again." In my first year, I died many times in front of my class. The last lines explain why I keep on teaching: "I keep on dying, / Because I love to live." I love to live, and to teach.

—*Jovan Miles*
High School Instructional Coach for math and science
Atlanta, Georgia

The Lesson

I keep on dying again.
Veins collapse, opening like the
Small fists of sleeping
Children.
Memory of old tombs,
Rotting flesh and worms do
Not convince me against
The challenge. The years
And cold defeat live deep in
Lines along my face.
They dull my eyes, yet
I keep on dying,
Because I love to live.

—*Maya Angelou*

Five years ago, I read Gregory Orr's volume of poetry a dozen times from cover to cover. My older brother had just died, and the tears came easily as I grasped for meaningful connection. Poetry such as Orr's was one of the few things that I could make sense of; the other was teaching.

It was the winter of my first year of teaching. And twenty smiling first graders greeted me each morning. As anybody who teaches knows, kids come whether you're ready or not, ecstatic or exhausted, revived or grieved. The kids who need you as their teacher are there each morning, asking for all you have to give. Some stay with you late into the evening, as their lives reverberate within you.

Indeed, as Orr puts it, a resurrection happens with every breath. I can well remember the first smile I was gifted, one from a child proud of his writing. I was then "reborn in a sacred part" of my body.

Recently, I pulled Orr's book from the shelf and remembered folding more than half of the hundred pages down in dog-ears as his words sang to me. I am struck now, as I was then, by the realization that our best days, the ones we aim for each morning, are those when we "hear the poem which is the world," and everything from the tear to the smiling mouth is possible. It is from there that I strive to teach, and it is there that my students take me.

—*John Mayer*
Elementary School Teacher
Portland, Oregon

It's not magic; it isn't a trick.
Every breath is a resurrection.
And when we hear the poem
Which is the world, when our eyes
Gaze at the beloved's body,
We're reborn in all the sacred parts
Of our own bodies:

                    the heart
Contracts, the brain
Releases its shower
Of sparks,

          and the tear
Embarks on its pilgrimage
Down the cheek to meet
The smiling mouth.

                —*Gregory Orr*

I will retire this year! It is a decision I have made. As I face retirement, I think back to how it all began—a dynamic mix of formal and informal education that took place at the height of the civil rights movement in Memphis, Tennessee.

When I first began teaching, Public Law 94-142, which would mandate public education for all children regardless of disability, had not yet been passed into law. I taught children with autism, and neither the children nor the programs that served them were recognized to be public education's responsibility. I began in a system that didn't consider me a "real teacher."

Throughout my teaching career, I have been passionate about helping others move from anxiety and fear to finding their own hunger and love for learning. I still feel the pull of that passion. The unknown terrain of *being retired* brought the fear that who I have been for the last thirty-eight years might somehow no longer be visible—that without my "work, activity" I might disappear. My head filled with questions driven by this new anxiety. But then Judy Sorum Brown's words enabled me to twist the energy of that fearfulness.

And now, as I imagine myself retired, my heart asks the question, *How will my passion for teaching manifest itself?* I know I must choose to stay visible, choose to show up, choose to reach out to those who come next. My small work in the greater work of the world is critical—it is my life's work. I am a *teacher.*

—*Sandie Merriam*

Retired Teacher of science and special education
North Myrtle Beach, South Carolina

Hummingbirds asleep

When do the hummingbirds
get naps? When do they sleep?
The tiny helicopter-birds,
buzzing about their busy business
all day long are nowhere to be found
at four fifteen
with dawn an hour away.

When they're at rest, they're gone.
Evaporated. They don't exist.
It's only busyness, activity
gives them their visibility,
their realness in our eyes.

Maybe we think the same of us.
Without our work,
activity,
we disappear,
Or so we fear.

—*Judy Sorum Brown*

I was privileged to go to schools that encouraged me to express the voice inside of me, to hone it, and to trust it. My teachers also taught me to listen well to the voices of others—to seek out my classmates' ideas and to consider them with and against my own as we engaged in discussion and debate. That is how we learned. Listening and talking held a central place in my thinking about what it would mean to teach children.

When I first started teaching in the Baltimore City Public Schools, it was distressing to see a version of teaching that emphasized independent worksheet learning rather than the discussions that defined my education. Now I aim to do for my fifth graders what my teachers did for me: to make the classroom a space and place for meaningful talk and exchange.

That is my challenge. I have to trust my inner "teacher's voice"—the voice that tells me that it is not just okay for me to deviate from the requisite script of the standardized curriculum, practice worksheets, and test preparation—it's necessary. Children learn when they can formulate, articulate, and revise their thoughts and theories, to themselves and with each other, in a caring and respectful classroom environment. And when they feel that someone "deeply listens" to their ideas and dreams, when they feel "understood" and "loved"—so much is possible.

—*Nell Etheredge*
Elementary School Teacher
Baltimore, Maryland

When Someone Deeply Listens to You

When someone deeply listens to you
it is like holding out a dented cup
you've had since childhood
and watching it fill up with
cold, fresh water.
When it balances on top of the brim,
you are understood.
When it overflows and touches your skin,
you are loved.

When someone deeply listens to you,
the room where you stay
starts a new life
and the place where you wrote
your first poem
begins to glow in your mind's eye.
It is as if gold has been discovered!

When someone deeply listens to you,
your bare feet are on the earth
and a beloved land that seemed distant
is now at home within you.

—*John Fox*

I first ran across this poem when my enthusiasm for teaching was waning. The passion and excitement that I had initially felt for teaching and reaching individual students were melting away, being replaced by the sensation that daily I was facing a formless, nameless mass of humanity.

Teachers have incredible power to hurt and to heal. But often we get overwhelmed by the monotony of the day-to-day life of the teacher—the paperwork, the grading, the endless forms to fill out, the reports to file, the lunchroom duties, the bus duties, the report cards to send home. We forget that the most important part of what we do is building and healing human beings, one at a time.

When I read this poem, I cried. It brought back into sharp relief what I had been forgetting: that teaching is an expression of love. Period.

So many times students come to us wounded—by parents, by former teachers, by peers, by the system, by life. Some wounds are visible, and some are not, but all of them could use a tender touch of understanding and compassion.

Much as Michelangelo saw the angel in the marble and carved until he set it free, Mr. Barta discerned the snowfall hidden in the paper left blank in an expression of resentment and frustration. I have a sign on my desk that reads, "See the snowfall." It serves as a reminder of my most important job as a teacher—and as a human being.

—*Leatha Fields-Carey*
High School English Teacher
Smithfield, North Carolina

Purple

In first grade Mrs. Lohr
said my purple teepee
wasn't realistic enough,
that purple was no color
for a tent,
that purple was a color
for people who died,
that my drawing wasn't
good enough
to hang with the others.
I walked back to my seat
counting the swish swish swishes
of my baggy corduroy trousers.
With a black crayon
nightfall came
to my purple tent
in the middle
of an afternoon.

In second grade Mr. Barta
said draw anything;
he didn't care what.
I left my paper blank
and when he came around
to my desk
my heart beat like a tom tom.
He touched my head
with his big hand
and in a soft voice said
the snowfall
how clean
and white
and beautiful.

—*Alexis Rotella*

This is not what I signed up for! This thought has popped up throughout my teaching career. It came up in my first year when I was fresh out of college and a disgruntled colleague told me I'd never make it past the first five years. But I persevered and made it to my third year of teaching, although I was then devastated when I lost a student to leukemia. Then, in my fourth year, my students and I witnessed the horrors of 9/11 from our classroom windows just a mile away from ground zero. Still I stayed.

Since I first started fifteen years ago, the demands and pressures have only intensified. Overcrowded classrooms. Shrinking budgets. Stressed-out teachers. High-stakes tests. These are the tragedies we face each day. But I knew that there would be challenges that came with the territory. A product of the New York City public school system, I have always felt a strong commitment to give back, and so I stayed.

What keeps me going is the "thread" that William Stafford describes in his poem. Now, more than ever, I know my role as an instructional coach is important, engaging teachers and students in the joys and wonder of learning together. I want to stay. I don't want to abandon the school system. This is the thread I signed up to follow.

And yet, having just given birth to my second child, I find myself at a crossroads. Stafford's poem reminds me that no matter what comes next, I must not let go of my thread.

—Donna Y. Chin

Literacy Coach and Teacher of English as a Second Language
New York, New York

The Way It Is

There's a thread you follow. It goes among
things that change. But it doesn't change.
People wonder about what you are pursuing.
You have to explain about the thread.
But it is hard for others to see.
While you hold it you can't get lost.
Tragedies happen; people get hurt
or die; and you suffer and get old.
Nothing you do can stop time's unfolding.
You don't ever let go of the thread.

—*William Stafford*

In my thirteenth year in the classroom, I fell out of love with teaching. Moving from a caring, progressive school to a so-called "failing" school, I lost my way as a teacher.

Previously free to craft my lessons, I was handed a stack of textbooks to follow exactly. I was informed that singing with my kindergarteners would "get me in trouble." I received similar messages about infusing my lessons with creative activities that would take us away from the prescribed curriculum. I felt tremendous pressure to "make" my kindergarteners learn more, faster. In my rush to cover the curriculum, I didn't take the time to build community and routines, and it showed. For the first time, I dreaded coming to work.

One day I "cheated" and read *Don't Let the Pigeon Drive the Bus*. My students came alive. I saw them in a way I had missed. I began talking with them more at recess and snack time. I started "conversation journals," letting them write to me each day and responding back each night. As we connected in more genuine ways, I remembered what I knew in my heart: I wasn't a teacher of curriculum, I was a teacher of children. Over time, I found ways to bend without breaking the rules and devised ways to meet my students' needs. These small moments rekindled my love of teaching.

Many teachers feel the loss of teaching as they imagined or once experienced it. I hope that like me, they can hold on to or rediscover their love of this "friend," our noble profession.

—Margaret Wilson
Middle School Language Arts Teacher
Riverside, California

I loved my friend.
He went away from me.
There's nothing more to say.
The poem ends,
Soft as it began,—
I loved my friend.

   —*Langston Hughes*

In this, my fifth year of teaching, I've already been shuffled around to various teaching positions—urban, rural, private, and public. I've striven for excellence in my profession, but I've also been laid off, had my salary cut, and been told that I've entered a career without promise. But like many of my fellow teachers who face similar situations, I just keep standing up—for myself, for my students, and for the integrity of my profession.

"The Real Work" brings with it a simple, ringing truth that echoes my experience: hardship inspires innovation, honesty, and a desire to persevere enough to fight through. It is when we reach a dead end that multitudes of previously unseen paths open up to meet us. Thinking back on my own teaching paths, I realize that I am my career's cartographer, drafting a map rich with color and experience.

The poem also makes me think of my students, many of whom shoulder unthinkable burdens, yet still manage to employ their mind and spirit in the journey of learning. Students show bravery every time they put their own voice to a page despite the uncertainty that can come from all directions, without and within.

So much of teaching is doing the work of standing back up—knowing with profound certainty that our "baffled minds" are meant to do this "real work" of journeying together, to teach our students and ourselves that the struggles we overcome help strengthen the voice of our song.

—Amy Harter
High School English and Theater Arts Teacher
Port Washington, Wisconsin

The Real Work

It may be that when we no longer know what to do
we have come to our real work,

and that when we no longer know which way to go
we have begun our real journey.

The mind that is not baffled is not employed.

The impeded stream is the one that sings.

—Wendell Berry

Using Poetry for Reflection and Conversation

When President Barack Obama visited South Africa in the summer of 2013, he visited Robbins Island prison, where Nelson Mandela was incarcerated for twenty-seven years. The president brought his daughters to the cell where Mandela was imprisoned. "Seeing them stand within the walls that once surrounded Nelson Mandela, I knew this was an experience they would never forget," Obama said.[1]

At a dinner with South African president Jacob Zuma, Obama then recited the poem "Invictus" that Mandela had read to the other Robben Island prisoners to sustain their courage and give them the fortitude to withstand the horrific and unjust conditions of their captivity. "It matters not how strait the gate, / How charged with punishments the scroll," Obama read. "I am the master of my fate: / I am the captain of my soul."

---

1. M. Shear, "Obama Visits Prison Cell That Helped Shape Modern South Africa," *New York Times*, June 30, 2013.

Obama's recognition of the power of this poem in Mandela's life speaks to poetry's capacity to touch the human soul and open up opportunities for us to retain our humanity. For Mandela and his fellow prisoners, the words of "Invictus" joined them together amid their punishing isolation and served as a talisman against hopelessness and despair.

Poetry, as Edward Hirsch wrote, "sacramentalizes experience."[2] It is in some way odd that mere words can have such an enduring impact, because unto itself, poetry exists as scratches on a page, spoken words, or pixels on a screen. The structure of this book illumines a potent alchemic exchange that occurs in the relationship between a poem and a reader. The commentaries highlight how, as the noted literary theorist Lois Rosenblatt contended, "A poem or a play remains merely inkspots on paper until a reader transforms them into a set of meaningful symbols."[3] The companion essays represent how teachers experience that encounter. Hirsch wrote of this meeting of reader and poem by quoting the great French poet Paul Celan, who said, "A poem, as a manifestation of language and thus essentially dialogue, can be a message in a bottle, sent out in the—not always greatly hopeful—belief that somewhere and sometime it could wash up on land, on heartland perhaps. Poems in this sense, too, are under way: they are making toward something."[4] This "something" results in a response of tension, insight, emotion, and sensation. It stirs us. As Hirsch concluded, "Imagine you have gone down to the shore and there, amidst the other debris—the seaweed and rotten wood, the crushed cans and dead fish—you find an unlikely looking bottle from the past. You bring it home and discover a message inside."[5]

---

2. E. Hirsch, *Poet's Choice* (Boston: Houghton Mifflin Harcourt, 2006), xv.

3. L. M. Rosenblatt, *Literature as Exploration* (repr., New York: Modern Language Association, 1938), 23.

4. Quoted in E. Hirsch, *How to Read a Poem: And Fall in Love with Poetry* (Boston: Houghton Mifflin Harcourt, 1999), 13.

5. Hirsch, *How to Read a Poem*, 1.

This section depicts those moments of uncorking the bottle. It describes practical, pragmatic, and procedural ideas for how to find your way to the "shore" with more frequency and structure. It shares the ideas, habits, and approaches to poetry suggested by educators. It is important to note that we focus not on the pedagogy of bringing poetry to students—that is beyond the scope of this book— but on how teachers use poetry in their own lives and in the practice of being a teacher.

Produce Your Own Version of Teaching with Heart

Since we published *Teaching with Fire* in 2003, we have heard from a number of readers who have adapted the structure and form of the book to generate reflection and discussion in classes, with their colleagues, and in their community. For example, one out-of-school program launched *Growing Up*, in which teenagers identified poems and song lyrics that were important to them and wrote commentaries that described the poems and lyrics significant to their lives. A high school English class did a similar assignment focused on poems and lyrics that "they read or listened to" by themselves; students then prepared a short presentation to the class that involved a reading of a poem or lyric and sharing their commentary.

This same process is also something that you can do with your colleagues or staff. We have led numerous sessions in which teachers have selected their favorite poems and commentaries from our books and read those aloud to each other. This can be a meaningful way to build community and shared meaning in a short period of time.

Here is the process in three steps:

1. Begin by sharing several story and poem combinations from *Teaching with Fire, Leading from Within,* or *Teaching with Heart*.

2. Structure the assignment using the following steps and prompts, which we developed in guiding our process for creating these books.

    *   Identify a poem that matters to you because it informs how you think about your identity as a teacher or your work in education.
    *   Write a brief commentary (up to 250 words) that describes your personal relationship with and connection to the poem. Your commentary should not be an explication, but a personal narrative that describes how this poem touched you and how it helps you make sense of your life and work as an educator. Several prompts that can help frame or direct your writing include:

        How did you discover the poem? What is the story behind your connection to this poem?

        What about this poem has remained meaningful to you?

        How do you "use" the poem to inform your work or your life?

        What do you notice or what has stood out to you from this poem, and how does it show up in your life? What do you sense this poem is trying to tell you?

        How does this poem help you clarify or explain what is important?

3. Provide an opportunity for a public exposition of the work, such as a printed book, a blog, or a reading.

Post Poetry Everywhere: At Home, in the Office, on Desks, on Walls . . .

Teachers do their work and live their lives amid words, language, stories, and poetry. Classroom walls; school hallways; books; assignment pages; handouts; and gifts for students, colleagues, and families are all places and spaces to fill up with poetry.

John Mayer, an elementary school teacher, has been known to "accidentally" leave a poem in the copier at school. He said that these poems are often found by appreciative audiences of other teachers or staff at school. The anonymity creates a buzz as the finder tries to discover who left the poem there. In showing the poem to others, he or she is indeed engaging with it in a fun way.

Melissa Madenski, a middle school writing teacher, wrote of the simple pleasure in giving something with no expectation of return: "I've written poems on napkins and left them for waiters, or tucked a poem in a library book for someone else to find. I invite students to write a poem in the sand next time they're at the beach. In China, poets write poems on concrete with water. When the water dries off the pavement, the poem is gone."

Angela Peery, a high school English teacher, keeps a framed copy of Ralph Waldo Emerson's "Success" in her office and a refrigerator magnet of it at home. She said it is one of her favorite poems for when she's feeling down about teaching.

Several educators referred to the Poem in Your Pocket Day program (www .poets.org/page.php/prmID/406) as a source for poetry. Principal Cordell Jones wrote that Poem in Your Pocket Day is a project that one of his teachers has been doing for the past few years, and the children love it. They post poems all over campus so that everyone can see and enjoy them.

Quick Ideas for Sharing Poetry

- Post poems on doors or file cabinets as reminders, inspiration, and invitations.

- Give poems as gifts to students at graduation; keep copies to hand out in your office.

- Send poems instead of holiday cards.

- Put poems on business-size cards to give to colleagues or students at special times.

- Decorate the school with large posters of poetry that exemplifies the important values of the school, such as diversity, respect, family, success, and so on.

- Open and close class sessions with readings; and when you read poetry, be lively and energetic—bring poetry alive!

- Create opportunities for students to perform their favorite poems as part of a classroom activity, a community event, a production, or a poetry slam.

- Ask families to share their favorite poems (especially traditional and cultural) with the students and the school.

- Bring poets into the school to do workshops, readings, and so on.

- Encourage local PTAs and PTOs to buy poetry books for all their teachers.

- Sponsor an art contest in which the piece of art is inspired by a favorite poem.

- Sign up your class for any of the many "poem a day" newsletters. Check out "Resources for Teaching and Poetry on the Web" later in this section for suggested sites.

Poetry in Service of Contemplation-in-Action

Teaching is work of high action and intensity. Classroom teachers and administrators spend their days engaged in multiple layers of interactions. In fact, studies of the classroom find that each day, teachers engage in more than a thousand interpersonal exchanges with students. The constant press of engagement leaves teachers feeling worn down and depleted, and they seek ways to replenish their energy and capacity for the intellectual and emotional labor that teaching comprises.

One way teachers attempt to maintain balance and adapt to the relational demands of the work is by adopting what Parker J. Palmer has called the *vacation approach* to life. Exhausted by activity, we take a little vacation to refresh ourselves, then we plunge back into action until we are exhausted again, then we take another vacation until we renew the energy to wear ourselves down once more—and on the cycle goes."[6] Palmer went on to describe how the inverse of such frenetic and defeating actions would be contemplation, and he pointedly explained that he was not proposing a version of contemplation or "vacation" that involved "sitting in a lotus position and chanting a mantra," but rather advocating opening space for "contemplation-in-action." By this he meant finding ways to engage in ongoing reflection on who we are and what we do that matters most—while we are engaged in the work. And by so doing, we can find a way to combat the harried nature of our days and bring some measure of rest and a sense of focus to our work.

The teachers described a range of approaches that enable poetry to be part of that integral process:

Kirsten Olson shared how poems help ground her and ready her for teaching:

Poems require me to be quiet, to slow down, and to focus. Reading a poem is an exercise in mindfulness; to breathe into the meaning of the poem and to follow the poet's images and shifts of meaning can calm me and take me to a place of simply being. I often read a poem just before class, to help center myself when I am in emotional turmoil, or to encourage myself to push deeper into the truth of a situation or to see the truth as a teacher. Poems like David Whyte's "All the True Vows" encourage me to greater interpersonal courage and honesty as a teacher, or help me remember what's important. Just before class, to read something like Franz Kafka's "Learn to Be Quiet" helps me be the teacher I'd like to be.

---

6. P. J. Palmer, *The Active Life: A Spirituality of Work, Creativity, and Caring* (San Francisco: Jossey-Bass, 1999), 16.

Sandie Merriam, a newly retired teacher, wrote that the poem she submitted for the book "has been my constant companion since my friend gave it to me. I have handwritten it into my grade book this year in order to keep it visible even in the last months of my career as a teacher."

Jay Casbon of Oregon State University uses poetry as a way to inspire him in tough times: "We all need as much inspiration and courage as we can muster in these very trying times. I use poetry as a kind of vitamin supplement for my spirit each and every day. It works!"

Capturing Attention

After winning the Pulitzer Prize for poetry, Mary Oliver wrote a short user's guide to poetry. She called it *A Poetry Handbook*. In it she describes how poems create "an *instance*—an instance of attention, of noticing something in the world."[7]

Jovan Miles, a high school math coach, wrote,

> Sometimes I write song lyrics, lines from a poem, quotes, or questions on a note card and use a paper clip to attach the note card to my shirt pocket. Students will walk up to me and ask me what my message means, and we'll have a short conversation about the message, why I chose it, and how it applies to school. It's an easy way for me to make students think deeply about something without my having to overtly bring it to their attention. I try to write things that will provoke a question, a laugh, a double take, or some other type of response that lets me know either that students "get" what I'm trying to say or that they want to "get" it.

---

7. M. Oliver, *A Poetry Handbook* (San Diego: Harcourt Brace, 1994), 74.

For example, Miles told us,

I once wrote, "You can pay for school but you can't buy class" on my note card and wore it around on my shirt pocket all day. The line was rapped by Jay Z on T. I.'s song "Swagga Like Us," which was a popular song when I taught eighth-grade math during the 2008–2009 school year. The eighth-grade students were often very rude to one another and to some of the new staff members, and I wanted to bring that to their attention without lecturing them or beating them over the head with admonitions about good behavior. I was able to teach them that good manners and socially acceptable behavior, or class, was something that had immense value to them as adolescents and would later be useful to them as adults. I was only able to do this because my "lesson" came in the form of a conversation initiated by the students.

Poetry among Colleagues

Teachers shared how they found poetry to be a powerful asset in intentionally creating space and practices hospitable to meaningful conversations. Poetry read and considered in a group helped start conversations between teachers and those they worked with and for in the school setting—students, colleagues, administrators, and parents.

Several teachers shared how poetry can help to open meetings or create a positive atmosphere for group work. Angela Peery wrote: "When I conduct meetings of an English department at a school, I often open meetings with a provocative poem and allow the teachers to speak to it in whatever fashion they wish. A useful resource for these poems is the Poetry 180 website (www.loc.gov /poetry/180/), where teachers can find a poem a day to use with high school students."

Jay Casbon shared how he used poetry to help draw out qualities he wanted in a team effort: "The poem I used to set the tone for an evaluation was Wendell Berry's 'Manifesto: The Mad Farmer Liberation Front.' I wanted to encourage and give permission for more courage, innovation, and risk taking in my role as a dean."

Principal David Hagstrom explained how he has selected and used poems to help his faculty think about specific issues, challenges, and possibilities. Poems have served as initiators of conversations or group processes:

As a "person encourager" (when I'm talking or listening to a person involved in a discernment process), I often use the little poem of Shel Silverstein's, "The Voice" (from *Falling Up*), in the conversation. As a "school coach" (when I'm attempting to help teachers find their "shared vision" and determine their next steps), I often use William Stafford's "The Way It Is." I use this poem with entire school groups because of my belief that a school's vision is not "created anew," it is "polished." I think that you have to look and listen for what's really important in the work that you do with children in your community, identify that fine work, and then move forward.

Jani Barker, who provides professional development, attested to the power of reading poems in workshops:

I will read poems during relevant moments throughout the workshop sessions. Usually a particular poem will help us support our pedagogy with conversations that include personal stories. A meaningful poem can take our dialogue from workshop theory into the realities of the classroom. This not only helps teachers construct new understandings but also helps them transfer this knowledge into their students' learning experiences.

I have been grateful and humbled when listening to teachers share their personal responses to various poems. A tangible change occurs when people in a group open their minds and hearts to each other's stories. We begin to understand that although our backgrounds may be different, there is a thread of trust forming. This trust allows us to extend our comfort level and reach out to new ways of seeing and understanding each other, the children we teach, and our pedagogy.

Others have used poetry books as a way to build community across large districts. In Fairfax, Virginia, where there are 230 Fairfax County schools and centers, John Marston helped organize an effort to give poetry books as gifts to teachers and arrange for book talks for lead mentor teachers. The Fairfax County Council of PTAs also hosted a book reading and posted the book on its website as its recommendation for a Teacher Appreciation Week gift. Working through such large systems is a great way to share poetry with many people.

Learn to Use Poems to Facilitate Conversations

Numerous educators described how they have used poetry to jump-start conversations or group processes. They described how they would introduce a poem and then launch a discussion. A key element of initiating and facilitating a conversation that uses poetry is first selecting the right poem and then having a range of open-ended questions or an activity to guide discussion.

Marcy Jackson, who prepares facilitators for the Center for Courage & Renewal programs, shared these ideas for initiating an activity with a poem:

- First, allow yourself to just sit with a poem. Read it through silently, then read it again—slowly, out loud.

- Let the poem's themes emerge for you. Enter the imagery. Notice the random thoughts and feelings that arise for you.

- Discover what this poem is saying to you—you personally. And then ask yourself what larger messages, themes, and questions are addressed in the poem.

- Jot down the questions that surface within you as you read the poem—questions about phrases, words, connections of one image to another, and surprising juxtapositions, or universal questions (you may choose to use some of these as "prompts" for conversation or journaling when you use the poem with a large group).

- Think about the ways that this poem connects with the larger themes or questions you want to work with—Where might it lead the group? How might it open things up for people? How will it move the conversation to a deeper place?

Other longtime facilitators also shared specific prompts that they have used along with a poem to engage others in reflection and discussion:

- What do you think the poem is about?

- Where does this poem intersect with your life or your background?

- What do you notice in this poem? What stood out to you?

- What image, sound, or phrase do you find yourself drawn to?

- What is happening in this poem, and to whom?

- What do you find elusive or opaque?

- What do you sense this poem is trying to tell you?

- Whom would you give this poem to, and why?

One of the "dangers" of using poetry in groups is that facilitators often try to churn through a process too quickly. Poetry can be intimidating, conjuring up bad memories of high school poetry encounters focused on dogmatic line-by-line explication. Several facilitators suggested that reading a poem and then providing time for group rumination are critical to engaging around poetry. One technique used involves asking participants to freewrite. In a freewriting exercise, participants read a poem and then are provided with an opportunity to write. Facilitators either supply prompts or encourage the writers to compose in a freewheeling and open way, just recording their feelings, responses, and sensations. Through the process of freewriting, participants can work through ideas in the poems and develop insights that they can share in discussion. After a freewrite, it can be effective to meet in small groups of two or three for writers to speak about what came up for them before returning to the larger group.

Sharing Poems at Important Moments of Transition

Many teachers shared how they use poetry to start things off in class and meetings, to segue between activities, or to bring something to a close. They described reading poems at transitions, such as when opening a classroom; including them in introductory letters home to families and students; and sharing them during public talks at graduation and other events. Poetry traffics in metaphor, and the compressed and intensified language triggers a response in those listening.

Michael L. Crauderueff, a high school Spanish teacher, shares poetry with his graduating seniors: "Along with a pot of rosemary, I always offer them a poem as a farewell gift. The Antonio Machado poem I have shared in this book—'Caminante'—is one I often give them, printed on beautiful paper with a beach and shoreline in the background. During our final Spanish class of the year, I ask my seniors to reflect on the days we have spent together and to savor those moments, as they will now begin to walk their own paths to the future."

Michael Poutiatine, professor of organizational leadership, uses poetry to shift a group's mind-set:

> I use poetry as a doorway into a new or hidden understanding, as a way to engage students to think differently about their work, their lives, and how they construct meaning. I rarely start classes with poetry. I am much more inclined to use a poem in the middle of a class to invite a shift in

thought patterns or structures. Or I will close a class with a poem that invites the students to leave with a different way of understanding a topic or conversation from what they came in with—food for thought as they walk out the door. Often these poems will resurface in later classes, brought back by the students for reconsideration.

Lianne Raymond teaches grades 11 and 12 and often has the same students for both years. "By the time they graduate, I know them pretty well. So for their last report card I find a quote or a poem that captures the spirit of the student and print it out on card stock, and then I write a personalized message on the back and include that with the report card. Students seem to really love them, many of them telling me years later that they still have it pinned up in their room."

Marianne Novak Houston, a retired middle school teacher, also has heard from a student how her experience of a poem stayed with her over time:

I used poems the students related to, and liked to invite them to write poems in the same "form" or "format" from their own perspective, from their own hearts. This proved to be fun and rather wonderful over the forty years I taught! Recently, I got a letter from a young woman who is today an attorney in Chicago. I hadn't heard from her since she finished sixth grade. She wrote to say hello and to tell me that the most important experience of her school life was in sixth grade when I invited the girls to write their own poem, after Rudyard Kipling's poem "IF." She sent me a copy of that writing and explained how she had tried to live up to what she'd written.

John J. Sweeney, elementary school teacher, spoke of how illustrating can provide another perhaps less intimidating way into poetry for someone of any age:

I like to give my students copies of poems printed on a page with space to illustrate. It really makes them look at the poem closely, think about what the poet is saying, and respond to the poem. This is useful for younger students because poetry can elicit feelings that are difficult for young students to verbalize. I suspect that this could be useful for readers of all ages, as it can be intimidating to attempt to respond to a poet's words with our own words. Illustrating also provides students with a personalized copy of a poem to cherish and can create a long-lasting connection to the piece.

Reading Poetry Out Loud

Rick Jackson, cofounder and senior fellow at the Center for Courage & Renewal, described the experience of listening to a poem read out loud:

> It is quite amazing to be sitting, silent and spellbound, in a large audience while listening to a poem being read. It is a way of being intellectually and spiritually intimate in public, of being, as Parker Palmer calls it, "alone together." And it is a wonderful way to connect across generations. A few years back, poet laureate Billy Collins came to Bainbridge Island, Washington, and read in a private home to a couple dozen people. When he returned two years later, he filled the Island Center Hall with two hundred eager listeners. And when he came the next year, he packed the high school gym with over a thousand—a standing-room crowd of all ages: elementary, middle, and high school youth, and adults of all races and walks of life. At some point during the reading, virtually everyone laughed and cried without hiding either. He helped us come closer together in community through the intimacy of words shared in public.

Robert Pinsky asserted not only that listening to poetry is a communal act but that live performance is the medium through which poetry should be experienced: "Reading a poem silently instead of saying a poem is like the difference between staring at sheet music or actually humming or playing the music on an instrument."[8] Michael Poutiatine described how he recites and performs poems in meetings:

> I only do this when the context calls for a "sage on the stage" approach. For me it becomes about reading the context and using some recitation for the purpose of inspiration. I have found it remarkably powerful if used at the right time in the right way, but I am also aware that it can backfire. The function of the use here is generally twofold. First it is about creating engagement, attention, interest; I find that a quality recitation can elicit a deeper engagement with material than can a simple reading (à la Poetry Out Loud). Second it is an invitation into me—to know me on a different level. So the poems I tend to choose are the ones that have deep resonance with me, the passionate resonance—the ones that give me chills or tears every time I read them.

Penny Gill, a college professor at Mount Holyoke, wrote: "At points of the semester when I just know the students will be weary and worn out, I take a poem in and just read it to them, telling them they need a little present." Liam Corley, currently an instructor at the US Naval Academy, wrote that he'd "found that the oral performance of poems enlivens discussions," suggesting the following link as a great source for such performances: www.favoritepoem.org/videos.html.

The Web and YouTube offer many opportunities to see and hear poems read out loud by many different voices and in a variety of styles—by the poets and spoken-word poets, as well as students and teachers. Hannah Cushing, a high school language arts teacher, recommended Button Poetry (http://buttonpoetry .com/) as a source for performance poetry. According to that website, "We seek to showcase the power and diversity of voices in our community. By encouraging and broadcasting the best and brightest performance poets of today, we hope to

---

8. Quoted in "Giving Voice to the American Audience for Poetry," accessed January 1, 2014, http://www .favoritepoem.org/principles.html.

broaden poetry's audience, to expand its reach and develop a greater level of cultural appreciation for the art form."

Resources for Teaching and Poetry on the Web

There are hundreds if not thousands of websites about poetry and teaching. And more will be launched each day. We can't possibly offer a comprehensive list here. Rather, we decided to ask our contributors to share some of their favorite websites and resources for teaching and poetry:

- **Bill Moyer's Fooling with Words** is "a PBS documentary special produced with young people in mind. We wanted them to see just how vital, compelling, and enjoyable poetry can be. So we took our cameras to the Geraldine R. Dodge Poetry Festival in Waterloo, New Jersey, to capture the excitement of 'the Woodstock of Poetry.' We covered the festival as if it were a sporting event, with cameras everywhere. . . The result is a film that will introduce your students to the power and pleasure of poetry in many guises." (www.pbs.org/wnet/foolingwithwords /main_video.html)
- **Favorite Poem Project (FPP)** showcases individuals reading and speaking personally about poems they love. As the FPP website notes: "One of the Favorite Poem Project's significant goals is to enhance and improve the teaching of poetry in the nation's elementary, middle and high school classrooms." For the last twelve years, Karen Harris, a contributor to this book, has served as the lead teacher for FFP's weeklong Summer Institute for Educators. The program gives teachers a chance to work with great poems; to learn with visiting poets like Louise Gluck, Mark Doty, and Rosanna Warren, along with resident poets Robert Pinsky and Maggie Dietz; and to be energized in their own work with fellow poet-inspired teachers. (www.favoritepoem.org)

- **Haiku.org** is hosted by the Haiku Society of America (HSA), which is "a not-for-profit organization founded in 1968 by Harold G. Henderson and Leroy Kanterman to promote the writing and appreciation of haiku in English. Membership is open to all readers, writers, and students of haiku. The HSA has been meeting regularly since its inception and sponsors open lectures, workshops, readings, and contests." (www.hsa-haiku.org/)

- **Poetry 180** is a site hosted by the Library of Congress. The poet Billy Collins introduces the site: "Poetry can and should be an important part of our daily lives. Poems can inspire and make us think about what it means to be a member of the human race. By just spending a few minutes reading a poem each day, new worlds can be revealed. Poetry 180 is designed to make it easy for students to hear or read a poem on each of the 180 days of the school year." (www.loc.gov/poetry/180/)

- **The Poetry Foundation,** "publisher of *Poetry* magazine, is an independent literary organization committed to a vigorous presence for poetry in our culture. It exists to discover and celebrate the best poetry and to place it before the largest possible audience." In addition, there is the foundation's Poetry Tool app, which lists poems by category and also connects to biographical information on the poets. (www.poetryfoundation.org)

- **Poetry Out Loud** "encourages the nation's youth to learn about great poetry through memorization and recitation. This program helps students master public speaking skills, build self-confidence, and learn about their literary heritage. Poetry Out Loud curriculum materials include the online poetry anthology, a comprehensive teacher's guide, a DVD of National Finals performances, lesson plans, and promotional and media guides." (www.poetryoutloud.org/teaching-resources/)

- **The Poetry Society of America,** "the nation's oldest poetry organization, was founded in 1910. Its mission is to build a larger and more diverse audience for poetry, to encourage a deeper appreciation of the vitality and breadth of poetry in the cultural conversation, and to place poetry at the crossroads of American life." (www.poetrysociety.org)

- **Poets.org,** in addition to spearheading Poem in Your Pocket Day, offers resources for teachers through an online poetry classroom: "Poets.org serves both as an interactive professional development program and a virtual community, enabling teachers across the country to access free poetry resources online. These teaching tools include innovative, classroom-tested curricula and discussion forums in which users can post strategies for and ask questions about teaching poetry at the primary, secondary, and university level." Under the tab "For Educators" there is a link to "Essays on Teaching," a wide range of essays written by students, teachers, and poets. (www.poets.org)

- **The Reading & Writing Project's** "mission is to help young people become avid and skilled readers, writers, and inquirers. We accomplish this goal through research, curriculum development, and through working shoulder-to-shoulder with students, teachers, principals and superintendents. The organization has developed state-of-the-art tools and methods for teaching of reading and writing, for using performance assessments and learning progressions to accelerate progress, and for literacy-rich content-area instruction." (http://readingandwritingproject.com/)

- **Shared Poetry Project** on the LearningMatters website "invites public school students to film community members reciting lines of poetry, then edit the readings into a video for the LearningMatters YouTube channel. This exciting project provides students the opportunity to develop or strengthen real-world skills of teamwork, quality control, and production. It also can introduce the 80% of Americans who do not have school-aged children to the remarkable abilities of our youth." (http://learningmatters.tv/blog/web-series/shared-poetry/9086/)

- **Teachers & Writers Collaborative** "seeks to educate the imagination by offering innovative creative writing programs for students and teachers, and by providing a variety of publications and resources to support learning through the literary arts." (www.twc.org)

- **The Writer's Almanac** features a poem a day read by Garrison Keillor. You can subscribe to receive daily poetry selections. (www.writersalmanac.org/)

Afterword

Sarah Brown Wessling

*R*eading the stories and poetry submitted by these far-flung colleagues moved me. Certainly they are full of passion and courage, doubt and tribulation, fortitude and tenacity. But really, what I heard was teachers describing softly, yet with resolve, a belief that too often the outside world overlooks: that the work of teaching changes lives.

Although profound, it is also a humble belief. Because at the center of all good teaching is a nexus of humility, an understanding that teaching isn't about the teacher, it's about the learner. Each of us who inhabits that teacher space serves to guide the learning journey of each student who walks through the door.

This sense of "teacher" isn't just one I came to through experience; it's also one that I inherited. When people ask me why I became a teacher, I tell them that it wasn't a decision, it was a realization of something that I must have always known. And I suppose I've always known that along with motherhood, teaching would be the thing I would share with my mother. My mother was *my* first teacher. She taught me about doing work you love and never just going to a job. She taught me that being a teacher isn't about being perfect, but about getting better. She taught me that we *never* stop learning, and that unconditional love is the gift that helps others discover and grow their passions. Everything that's good about me in the classroom today has some link to her, to her classroom, to how she lived "teacher."

For me, this book is another thread. It weaves the voices of so many poets who have anchored my own literary life and my curriculum with teacher voices that inspire me. It reminds me of my own purpose and reinvigorates my passion for teaching, which teems with the belief that nothing liberates like learning.

Sarah Brown Wessling is a high school English teacher at Johnston High School in Johnston, Iowa, where she has taught since 1998. In 2010 she was selected as the National Teacher of the Year and spent the year traveling the country and world as an ambassador for education. She is also the teacher laureate for Teaching Channel and is the host of the PBS series *Teaching Channel Presents*. She is also coauthor of the book *Supporting Students in a Time of Core Standards: English Language Arts, Grades 9–12*. Sarah continues to write, speak, and teach throughout the country while still answering the call to return to the classroom.

CENTER FOR
Courage
&Renewal

---

*T*he mission of the Center for Courage & Renewal is to create a more just, compassionate, and healthy world by nurturing personal and professional integrity and the courage to act on it.

For such a world, we need people—like the teachers in this book—who embrace their role and work together to solve pressing, complex problems. Courage & Renewal programs help individuals "lead from within" by acting with courage on their true callings, developing trustworthy relationships, sustaining themselves and others for the long haul, and working together to transform the institutions and communities they serve.

Founded in 1997 by author, activist, and educator Parker J. Palmer, the Center's approach was initially created to renew and sustain educators, and today also reaches those in health care, in ministry, and across communities.

Through its network of more than two hundred Courage & Renewal facilitators across North America and the globe, the Center offers online resources and in-person retreats and programs to cultivate the heart and soul of leadership.

Royalties from *Teaching with Heart* support the Center for Courage & Renewal and help more people effect positive change in the world.

Join this growing movement at www.CourageRenewal.org.

Center for Courage & Renewal
1402 Third Avenue, Suite 709
Seattle, WA 98101
206-466-2055
info@couragerenewal.org

The Contributors

Safaa Abdel-Magid has been teaching elementary-level classes in the Khartoum International Community School in Khartoum, The Sudan, for four years. She was born and raised in Sudan, attended college in the United States, and moved back to Sudan after she finished college.

Richard H. Ackerman, a former school teacher and administrator, is a professor of educational leadership at the University of Maine. He is the coauthor of *The Wounded Leader: How Real Leadership Emerges in Times of Crisis.*

Nina Ashur has been an educator for more than thirty years in public schools, a community college, and a private university. Currently she is an associate professor and director of the Learning Enrichment Center at Azusa Pacific University, where for nineteen years she has coordinated a variety of academic support services and taught undergraduates.

Will Bangs is a middle school humanities teacher in Northampton, Massachusetts. He is a proud recipient of the Pioneer Valley Teacher of Excellence award. When he is not teaching, he's usually hanging out with his family or writing music.

Mark Bielang has been superintendent of Paw Paw Public Schools in Michigan since 1995. Prior to that he was a high school principal, assistant principal, and teacher. In 2009–2010 he served as president of the American Association of School Administrators.

Hugh Birdsall began teaching high school French in 1977. Since 1995 he has taught English to speakers of other languages at the Regional Multicultural Magnet School in New London, Connecticut. Since 2001 he has also served on the summer faculty at the School for International Training in Brattleboro, Vermont.

Sandi Bisceglia is the executive director of the International Network of Principals' Centers (INPC), originally founded at Harvard University, and past president of the Florida Association of School Administrators. As a twenty-three-year pre-K–8 public school principal emeritus, she now spends her time creating "conversation venues for school leaders" through INPC and the website http://southernmostleadershipnetwork.com.

Rachel Boechler is the superintendent of schools in the Fox Point–Bayside School District in Milwaukee, Wisconsin. Previously, for five years she was the chief operating officer at CPS Human Resource Services in Sacramento, California. Her career spans twenty-nine years in various roles in K–12 education. Rachel has been engaged in the work of the Center for Courage & Renewal for over twelve years.

Jennifer Boyden taught creative writing, literature, and composition for nearly twenty years at various places, including Walla Walla Community College, Whitman College, and Soochow University in China. She also teaches independent and interdisciplinary, collaborative writing workshops. She is the author of *The Mouths of Grazing Things* and *The Declarable Future*.

Annette Breaux is an education speaker, author, and consultant. A former classroom teacher, curriculum coordinator, and teacher induction coordinator, she is the author of the best-selling *101 Answers for New Teachers and Their Mentors*. She has also coauthored books with both Harry Wong and Todd Whitaker.

Emily Brisse has worked as an English teacher for nine years at Minnesota's Watertown-Mayer High School. She earned her master of fine arts degree from Vermont College of Fine Arts, and loves teaching creative writing best.

Judy Sorum Brown teaches leadership for the public good through the School of Public Policy at the University of Maryland. She is also a writer and a poet. Her latest book is *The Art and Spirit of Leadership*.

Caridad Caro has been an educator in New York City public schools since 1995, teaching at Fannie Lou Hamer Freedom High School for twelve years. She is currently at the Urban Assembly School for Wildlife Conservation in the Bronx as a founding assistant principal.

Ruth Charney cofounded Northeast Foundation for Children and Responsive Classroom. She taught students from kindergarten through high school for over thirty-five years and worked with classroom teachers and school leaders to effect progressive change. She authored several books, including *Teaching Children to Care*.

Donna Y. Chin is a literacy coach and teacher of English as a second language at Shuang Wen School (P.S. 184) in Lower Manhattan. She has been teaching and coaching in the New York City public school system for fourteen years. She lives with her family in Jackson Heights, Queens.

Amy Christie taught third grade in New York City through Teach For America in 2001. In 2006 she founded and directed the college office at the Bronx Lab School. Currently she is the network director of college for Achievement First Public Charter Schools.

Kayleigh Colombero received her bachelor's degree from Smith College and her master's degree from Western New England University. She taught middle school and high school English and history for four years. She is currently the director of Project Coach and coordinator of urban education for Smith College.

Liam Corley has taught for about fifteen years. He is an associate professor of English at California State Polytechnic University, Pomona. Liam is spending 2013 to 2016 on military leave to serve as an instructor at the US Naval Academy. He is a veteran of Operation Enduring Freedom (Afghanistan).

Michael L. Crauderueff has been a language teacher for thirty-five years, and is currently teaching high school Spanish and peace studies at Friends' Central School in Wynnewood, Pennsylvania.

Hannah Cushing is embarking on her eighth year of teaching high school language arts. Currently she has the honor to spend her days learning with and from the students at West High School, a setting IV emotional and behavioral disorders program in Minnetonka, Minnesota.

Vicki Den Ouden has worked as an elementary school classroom, learning assistance, and reading intervention teacher for almost thirty years. After completing her master's degree, she also taught university courses in literacy education. She resides in Kelowna, British Columbia, Canada.

Kent Dickson is a professor of Spanish and Latin American literature at California State Polytechnic University, Pomona. Previously he was a middle and high school teacher of Spanish in North Hollywood, California. He has been a teacher for eighteen years.

Brian Dixon is the founder of the Mentorship Academy, a project-based public charter school in Baton Rouge, Louisiana. He helps classroom teachers and school administrators with practical strategies to prepare today's students for the changing world of tomorrow.

Nell Etheredge is a Teach For America (TFA) corps member teaching fifth grade in Baltimore City Public Schools. Before joining TFA, Nell was a legislative policy analyst with the Council of State Governments in Washington, DC, working in the areas of education and health policy.

Rachel Fentin is a first-year teacher in Detroit. She teaches fourth grade at University Prep Academy–Mark Murray.

Leatha Fields-Carey has taught in North Carolina in Johnston County Schools for twenty years. She currently teaches English and serves as the testing coordinator for Johnston County Middle College High School, a nontraditional public high school in Smithfield, North Carolina.

Lily Eskelsen García is vice president of the National Education Association. She began as a school lunch lady, became a kindergarten aide, and then became a sixth-grade teacher. Nine years later, she was named Utah Teacher of the Year. She is one of the country's most influential Hispanic educators.

Maureen Geraghty has been teaching for over twenty years. Fifteen of those years have been in some type of alternative school setting. She is a published writer/poet who is greatly involved with the Oregon Writer's Project. She lives in Portland, Oregon.

Kathleen Glaser has over thirty years' experience in public schools, serving as a teacher, principal, and college professor. She is a Center for Courage & Renewal facilitator, received the Washington Post Distinguished Educational Leadership Award, and is a cofounder of the Chesapeake Public Charter School in southern Maryland.

Mel Glenn retired in 2001, after teaching thirty-four years of high school English. He is the author of twelve books for young adults, including *Jump Ball*, *Split Image*, and *Who Killed Mr. Chippendale?* and speaks across the country at conferences and schools. His website is www.melglenn.com.

David S. Goldstein is a senior lecturer at the University of Washington Bothell, where he has taught for fifteen years, and also serves as director of its Teaching and Learning Center. He is the recipient of the University of Washington Distinguished Teaching Award. His research and writing lie in the scholarship of teaching and learning as well as in ethnic American literature.

Veta Goler is arts and humanities division chair and associate professor of dance at Spelman College in Atlanta, Georgia. She has been a dancer and dance teacher for over thirty-five years. She is also a national Circle of

Trust facilitator and leads retreats and workshops with the Center for Courage & Renewal.

Ronald Gordon has been teaching for forty years. He is full professor of communication at the Hilo campus of the University of Hawai'i. He teaches senior-level courses in listening, dialogue, and leadership, and is the author of *On Becoming an Attuned Communicator* and *Actualizing: Mindsets and Methods for Becoming and Being*.

Julie A. Gorlewski is assistant professor in the Department of Secondary Education at the State University of New York at New Paltz. In addition to serving as a parent advocate and education activist, she taught English in grades 7 through 12 for fifteen years. She has written several books and coedited *Using Standards and High-Stakes Testing* for *Students: Exploiting Power with Critical Pedagogy*.

Glendean Hamilton is a recent graduate of Smith College. She was a student teacher during the time of her commentary. Prior to that, she had numerous teaching internships while in college. In 2013 she began teaching sixth-grade English language arts in Lawrence Public Schools, Massachusetts.

Karen Harris is a lead teacher at the Favorite Poems Project's Summer Institute for Educators and an English teacher at Brookline High School. She is the mother of two children, and guitarist, songwriter, and singer for the rock band the Vivs. She lives in Arlington, Massachusetts.

Amy Harter is in her fifth year of teaching. She currently works at Sheboygan Falls High School in Wisconsin, teaching sophomore and senior English, Advanced Placement literature, and theater arts. She maintains a professional, reflective teaching blog at www.universeastext.com, and looks forward to the rest of her career journey.

David Henderson has been involved in pre-K–12 education for over twenty years. He currently teaches educational leadership at Montana State University in

Bozeman, and serves as a facilitator with the Center for Courage & Renewal. He continues to study and research the intersection of the inner life of leaders with their practice of leadership.

Mary Beth Hertz has been teaching in Philadelphia since 2002. She is certified in four different areas and holds a master's degree in instructional technology. She was named an ISTE Emerging Leader in 2010, and in 2013 was PAECT Outstanding Teacher of the Year and an ASCD Emerging Leader.

Julia Hill began teaching in 1998 with one trial-by-fire year with Teach For America in the Mississippi Delta. In the time since, she has pursued her passion for bringing progressive educational philosophy to urban communities from Minneapolis to the South Bronx and currently works as a reading specialist in St. Paul, Minnesota.

Kevin Hodgson has been teaching sixth grade for ten years at the William E. Norris Elementary School in Southampton, Massachusetts. He is also the technology liaison with the Western Massachusetts Writing Project and writes regularly about teaching and composition on his blog, *Kevin's Meandering Mind* (http://dogtrax.edublogs.org).

Dennis Huffman has been program director of Prince George's Community College at University Town Center in Hyattsville, Maryland, since 2000. He grew up on an Ohio apple farm and holds a master's degree in teaching English as a second language and a doctorate in community college education from George Mason University.

Christine Intagliata spent thirty years as a freelance writer and producer of nonfiction television and videos. She is working toward a dual master's in elementary education and special education with the Urban Teacher Center, a clinical master's program that trains teachers and places them in urban schools. She is a teaching resident in the second grade at Wheatley Education Campus in Washington, DC.

Gregory John has worked in education for twenty-six years—as a teacher, educational leader, and for the last eleven years as a school principal. He now serves students as a principal at Starr King Elementary School in San Francisco, where students from all walks of life come to learn how to read, write, think, and navigate their differences with grace.

Katie Johnson has taught in primary grades in Maine and Washington for thirty years. She has published books about writing (*Doing Words, More Than Words,* and *Reading into Writing*) and about movement and vision (*Red Flags for Primary Teachers*). Leaning more toward poetry lately, she admires Billy Collins and Valerie Worth.

LouAnne Johnson is a teacher and the author of several books, including *Dangerous Minds, Teaching Outside the Box, Kick-Start Your Class,* and the young-adult novel *Muchacho*. She also writes for young readers under the pen name Alyce Shirleydaughter. Her website is www.louannejohnson.com.

Cordell Jones has worked at all three levels of schools (elementary, middle, and high school) since 1993. Currently he is principal of Alamo Heights Junior School in San Antonio, Texas; an adjunct faculty member of Trinity University; and executive board member of the School Leaders Network.

Nora Landon has been teaching English to sophomores and seniors for over eight years, beginning at Oakwood Friends School in Poughkeepsie, NY. She is currently a member of the faculty at William Penn Charter School in Philadelphia, Pennsylvania.

Stephen Lazar is a National Board Certified history teacher who cofounded Harvest Collegiate High School in New York City. He works with teachers across the city and the nation to support inquiry-based instruction, project-based learning, and Common Core State Standards implementation.

Melissa Madenski began teaching in 1971, the first year women could wear pants in the public schools in her district. Currently she teaches writing to middle school students and adults.

Stephen Mahoney has been a teacher and a principal for twenty-five years. In 2005 he started the Springfield Renaissance School, an expeditionary learning mentor school in Springfield, Massachusetts, for students in grades 6 through 12. Renaissance teachers and students have proved that your ZIP Code does not have to be your destiny.

Rob Maitra is director of programs at Harlem RBI. Previously, he was a New York City public school teacher; a teacher education professor at Bryn Mawr College, Hunter College, and Teachers College, Columbia University; and director of educational advancement at the Boys' Club of New York.

Holly Masturzo serves as professor of humanities and English at Florida State College at Jacksonville. For twenty years she has taught in a variety of settings—at a research university, a historically black college, and a range of community sites. Her approach to arts learning appears in essays in *Third Mind: Creative Writing and Visual Art* and *The Alphabet of the Trees: A Guide to Nature Writing.*

John Mayer has taught first and second grade at Catlin Gabel School in Portland, Oregon, for six years, after studying for a master of arts in teaching from Lewis and Clark College. Before moving to Portland, he began his teaching career as a preschool teacher in Washington, DC, and considers himself very lucky to work with the brilliance of young minds.

Kathleen Melville has been teaching for nine years. She currently teaches English and Spanish at a small public high school in Philadelphia. Kathleen promotes teacher leadership with Teachers Lead Philly.

Sandie Merriam is a thirty-eight-year veteran science and special education teacher at North Myrtle Beach Middle School in Little River, South Carolina. She has been an advocate for youth empowerment in the areas of racial equity, justice education, service learning, and parent-school partnerships.

Tom Meyer began teaching in public high schools in 1986. Currently he is an associate professor of secondary education at the State University of New York at New Paltz. He directs the Hudson Valley Writing Project (a site of the National Writing Project), a lively network of teachers working together to improve literacy and writing instruction in the Hudson Valley.

Jovan Miles is a nine-year veteran of public education in Atlanta, Georgia. He currently works as an instructional coach supporting math and science teachers in the Atlanta public school system. His professional interests include culturally relevant pedagogy, public education as a tool for social justice, and early childhood education.

Dan Mindich is a teacher and administrator at Punahou School in Honolulu, Hawai'i. In his over twenty years of teaching in public and private schools, team teaching has been central to Dan's work, and he recently completed his doctoral dissertation looking at teacher learning communities.

April Niemela has thirteen years of experience in seventh- through twelfth-grade English language arts classrooms, and has witnessed seismic changes in the world of education. She is currently a curriculum resource teacher, charged with providing teachers with professional development and mentoring new educators.

Teri O'Donnell is a high school biology teacher in Northern California. For twenty years she has taught all grades from seventh through twelfth and every level from middle school life science to Advanced Placement biology. She is a founding member of her high school, now in its seventeenth year, and serves as science department chairperson.

Cindy O'Donnell-Allen is a full professor in the English department at Colorado State University (CSU) and director of the CSU Writing Project. She was a secondary-level teacher in Oklahoma for eleven years and wrote *Tough Talk, Tough Texts: Teaching English to Change the World*. She serves on the National Writing Project board of directors.

Kirsten Olson is a founding member of the Institute for Democratic Education in America (IDEA), a national activist organization that aims to transform education through local organizing, and author of *Wounded by School*. Prior to this, she was a university instructor for eleven years.

Alison Overseth is the executive director of the Partnership for After School Education (PASE), a nonprofit that works with over 1,600 community-based youth-serving agencies to improve the quality of after-school education programs available to young people living in poverty in New York City.

Emanuel Pariser cofounded in 1973 the Community School for students who have failed to thrive in high school, and codirected the school until 2006. In 2011 he cofounded Maine's first charter school: the Maine Academy of Natural Sciences in Hinckley, Maine, an agricultural and forestry-themed school for students who have been marginalized in conventional education.

Tiffany Poirier is an elementary school teacher and speaker who believes in the infinite gifts of every child. She is the author of *Q Is for Question: An ABC of Philosophy* (www.qisforquestion.com) and the founder of the Teaching Coats Project. Tiffany teaches online courses at Richer Learning, and she lives and works in Surrey, British Columbia, Canada.

Michael Poutiatine has taught and administrated in traditional and nontraditional schools, public, private, and independent, for over twenty-five years, with students from the middle school level to the doctoral candidate level. He currently teaches leadership at Gonzaga University in Spokane, Washington, and works with several school reform initiatives based in Washington State.

Wanda S. Praisner has taught for twenty-nine years at the elementary school level as well as in continuing education courses and adult writing workshops. She is currently a poet-in-residence for the New Jersey Writers Project, cosponsored by Playwrights Theater and the New Jersey State Council on the Arts.

Jamie Raskin is a professor of constitutional law at American University Washington College of Law, a Maryland state senator, and majority whip of the Maryland Senate. He is founder of the Marshal Brennan Constitutional Literacy Project and author of several books, including *We the Students*, which examines the Supreme Court's treatment of America's high school students.

Lianne Raymond has taught for twenty years in both middle and high school classrooms. She currently teaches grades 11 and 12 in psychology at Mark R. Isfeld Secondary School in Courtenay, British Columbia, Canada.

Kenneth Rocke is the director for the Pioneer Valley District and School Assistance Center. His team works with teachers, coaches, and administrators in schools throughout Western Massachusetts. A retired superintendent, he began his career in education teaching mill and house carpentry at Franklin County Technical School.

Susan Rodgerson graduated from the Art Institute of Boston at Lesley University and founded Artists For Humanity in 1991. She has received many awards, including an honorary doctorate from Tufts University (2008); the Massachusetts College of Art and Design Award for Excellence in Education (2006); and Social Entrepreneur in Residence from Pace University (2005).

Kaitlin Roig teaches first grade at Sandy Hook Elementary in Newtown, Connecticut. She has taught for seven years. Knowing that positive social change was needed, Kaitlin founded Classes 4 Classes (www.classes4classes .org), a nonprofit organization that enables K–5 students to learn compassion and kindness through exchanges with other schools.

Laura Roop is the director of outreach at the University of Michigan School of Education. She directed the Oakland Writing Project, a National Writing Project site, for sixteen years. In 1981 she began working as a high school English teacher, county-level language arts consultant, and state-level networking specialist.

Larry Rosenstock is CEO and founding principal of High Tech High (www .hightechhigh.org), a network of thirteen K–12 public charter schools in California, and is dean of the High Tech Graduate School of Education. He taught carpentry, served as an attorney at the Harvard Center for Law and Education, and directed the federal New Urban High School Project.

Tim Ryan is a congressman in his sixth term serving the Ohio Thirteenth Congressional District, which includes Youngstown, Warren, Akron, and Kent. He is a relentless advocate for increased investments in and improvements to American education and author of *A Mindful Nation: How a Simple Practice Can Help Us Reduce Stress, Improve Performance, and Recapture the American Spirit*.

Leanne Grabel Sander has received funding for an illustrated children's book, *The Little Poet*, and is working on a new spoken-word greatest hits show—*Call Them Jewels*. She has thirty years' experience as a poet and writer and eleven as a special education/language arts teacher.

Harriet Sanford is the president and CEO of the NEA Foundation and has led the work of the foundation since 2005. She began her career as a public school teacher, which led to a senior executive career of more than twenty-eight years, with twenty-two as president and CEO of nonprofit and public organizations.

Dena Simmons was raised by a resilient mother who escaped Antigua to come to the United States. After graduating with honors from Middlebury College, she returned to the Bronx as a middle school teacher. She is studying for her doctorate of education at Teachers College, Columbia University, where her research is on teacher preparedness as it relates to bullying in the middle school setting.

Thomas A. Stewart was an English teacher in Kentucky for ten years. After two years with the Kentucky Department of Education, he was a public school district administrator for five years. He teaches for Austin Peay State University's College of Education and is cofounder of Contemplative Learning Solutions Educational Consulting.

Paola Tineo first became involved with education through her own experience growing up in urban cities throughout the Northeast. She taught Spanish for a few years at a Boston public charter school and has recently moved to teach English as a second language in a district charter school in Dorchester, Massachusetts.

Lori Ungemah taught high school English in Brooklyn for eleven years. She is currently a founding faculty member of Guttman Community College at the City University of New York, where she is an assistant professor of English.

Tom Vander Ark is the author of *Getting Smart: How Digital Learning Is Changing the World* and CEO of Getting Smart (http://gettingsmart.com/). He is a partner in Learn Capital and was executive director of education for the Bill & Melinda Gates Foundation and a public school superintendent.

Jose Vilson is an educator, Web designer, speaker, and writer at TheJoseVilson.com. He has been featured on Edutopia, GOOD, CNN, and TEDx, and sits on the board of directors for the Center for Teaching Quality. You can find him at www.thejosevilson.com.

Ron Walker is a founding member and the founding executive director of the Coalition of Schools Educating Boys of Color. He has forty-five years' experience as a principal, vice principal, and middle school teacher and a passion for the affirmative development of all students—especially male students of color.

Randi Weingarten has been president of the American Federation of Teachers (AFT) since 2008. She previously headed New York City's United Federation of Teachers. She initiated the AFT's Quality Education Agenda, which advances reforms grounded in evidence, equity, scalability, and sustainability to reclaim the promise of public education.

Rachel Willis began teaching in 2004 through Teach For America. She was the 2009 Atlanta Public Schools Elementary Teacher of the Year and a Milken Educator Award recipient in 2010. She is currently director of teacher and alumni leadership development for Teach For America in the Washington, DC, region.

Margaret Wilson was a classroom teacher for fifteen years, and also taught at the University School of Nashville in Tennessee and in the San Bernardino City Unified School District in California. She is currently leaving Responsive Classroom to become the assistant head of a school and a teacher in Riverside, California.

Andy Wood has taught and coached at the high school level since moving to the United States from England in 2005, and served for three years as the program director of Project Coach, building capacity in urban youth through coaching and leadership opportunities. He currently teaches social studies at Northampton High School in Massachusetts and is the varsity boys' soccer coach.

Jane Zalkin recently retired, after almost thirty-five years of teaching four- and five-year-old children in neighborhoods with residents of very low socioeconomic status outside of Charleston, South Carolina. She was teaching the children and even grandchildren of her first students by the time she retired.

The Editors

Sam M. Intrator is the principal of the Smith College Campus School and professor of education and child study at Smith College. The son of two retired New York City public school teachers, Sam co-founded and currently codirects Project Coach—a nationally recognized and replicated youth development program in Springfield, Massachusetts, that prepares high school students to be youth sports coaches and run leagues and tutoring programs for elementary-age children. He was awarded a W. K. Kellogg National Leadership Fellowship and was named a Distinguished Teacher by the White Commission on Presidential Scholars. He is the coauthor of *The Quest for Mastery: Positive Youth Development through Out-of-School Programs* and *Tuned In and Fired Up: How Teaching Can Inspire Real Learning in the Classroom*, the editor of *Stories of the Courage to Teach: Honoring the Teacher's Heart*, and the coeditor of *Leading from Within: Poetry that Sustains the Courage to Lead* and *Teaching with Fire: Poetry That Sustains the Courage to Teach*.

Megan Scribner has nearly thirty years of experience editing books, essays, and reports. She primarily works as an editor and author coach, helping authors find the best way to communicate their ideas and making sure their voice comes through loud and clear. She has edited over twenty-five books, essays, and guides, including, most recently, *Transformative Conversations: A Guide to Mentoring Communities among Colleagues in Higher Education*, *The Art and Spirit of Leadership*, and *The Transforming Leader: New Approaches to Leadership for the Twenty-First Century*. With Parker J. Palmer and Arthur Zajonc, she coauthored

The Heart of Higher Education: A Call to Renewal, and with Parker J. Palmer, she coauthored the tenth-anniversary edition of *The Courage to Teach Guide for Reflection and Renewal*. With Sam M. Intrator, she also coedited *Leading from Within: Poetry That Sustains the Courage to Lead*, and *Teaching with Fire: Poetry That Sustains the Courage to Teach*. She has also taken on various leadership roles in local schools through the PTA and in her community as an organizer and facilitator on environmental and community issues.

Gratitudes

The last poem in this volume is Wendell Berry's "The Real Work." It begins, "It may be that when we no longer know what to do / we have come to our real work." In assembling this book, we lived that moment of "not knowing." It hit us as we sat at Megan's kitchen table with a binder spilling over with hundreds of submissions. Each submission included a cherished poem accompanied by a story of what it means to work and live as a teacher.

Our job was to select ninety narratives and poems of teachers doing "real work," and it was daunting. As we concluded what was an agonizing process, we realized that we could have created three distinct volumes, each offering a perspective on the real work of teaching.

To those hundreds of submitters—thank you for your courage to share a glimpse of your heart and what matters most to you as an educator. We are particularly grateful to those who, on finding out they were not accepted, still responded with generosity and good wishes for the success of the book. To those ninety submitters who are in the book, thank you for your willingness to work with us around the countless revisions and for responding to our requests for more sources and stories about how you use poetry.

The poet most submitted by teachers was Emily Dickinson. She is known as the "solitary poet" because she rarely left her home in Amherst, Massachusetts, and almost never shared any of the nearly eighteen hundred poems she reportedly composed. The irony of Dickinson's popularity is that she embodies the cloistered artist working to her own isolated muse, whereas this book and project exists because of an engaged and devoted community working together. We would like to thank those whose work and efforts moved this project from idea to production.

Parker J. Palmer and Taylor Mali open the book by honoring the teacher's heart and celebrating the noble work of the profession. Sarah Brown Wessling brings the book to a close by evoking an image of teaching across the generations. In their work, all three bring great heart and hope to teachers across the country. To the team at the Center for Courage & Renewal: you work tirelessly to develop approaches for nurturing personal and professional integrity. Special thanks to Terry Chadsey, Rick Jackson, Marcy Jackson, Shelly Francis, and Robin Gaphni. To our colleagues at Jossey-Bass who believe that books should move the spirit: Lesley Iura, Nana Twumasi, Robin Lloyd, Francie Jones, Tracy Gallagher, and Amy Reed, thanks for all your support and faith in this book. To Sheri Gilbert, thanks for your great patience with the permissions process and your careful attention to detail.

Sam writes: I am blessed to be surrounded by so many people whose "real work" involves lifting up others: Tom and Betsy Coghlin, Rob Kunzman, Maureen Litwin, Marlene Musante, Don and Sharon Siegel, and Jo Glading DiLorenzo. To my own family: Jake, you have always found strength and magic in words, story, and poetry. Kaleigh, so many depend on you; you are a true buddy. Casey, I think of "Invictus" when I think of your journey and how you go forward. Riley, if there is a genre called action poetry, it is for you. Finally, Jo-Anne, you embody the essence of this heroic profession.

Megan writes: I am so fortunate that editing books such as this one is my "real work." It is an honor to collaborate with so many dedicated and inspiring educators—working with them has been a real pleasure. Many thanks to my family, good friends, and community who keep me energized and hopeful. Special thanks to my parents, sister, and brother, the love and resilience of our family are true gifts. To my daughters: I delight in who you are and will become. Anya, your heart and talents will take you far, and Maya, your exuberance and spirit know no bounds. And Bruce, you are wise and wonderful; your love, friendship, and support mean the world to me.